A DUKE STREET BOYHOOD
growing up in Chelmsford, 1910-1918

Basil Harrison

edited by
Prue James

IAN HENRY PUBLICATIONS

ISBN 0 86025 522 0

The photograph on the cover is of
Basil Harrison, just before he retired

Published by
Ian Henry Publications, Ltd.
20 Park Drive, Romford, Essex RM1 4LH
and printed by
Interprint, Ltd.
Industrial Estate, Marsa, Malta

PREFACE

The following is based on the observations and memories of my father, Basil Harrison, who was born in the centre of Chelmsford at the beginning of the twentieth century. It is the story of a small boy growing up in the bustling and lively environment of Duke Street, of everyday occurrences which were of interest to him, of happenings which were exciting to him and of unique events which remained etched on his memory for the remainder of his eighty-six years.

Many of my father's recollections are taken from what he referred to as his 'Jottings'. Those dating back to the 1950s are written neatly in either sentence or note form. In his later years, when he felt that time was running out, he simply jotted down odd notes on the back of old envelopes or scraps of paper. Thus he refers to events as having happened fifty, seventy or perhaps eighty years before.

Sadly, Father's eyesight failed in his eighties. For one who loved to read this was a cruel blow but, on the credit side, it gave him more time for reminiscing with family and friends. It was during this period that I heard so much about his childhood and the way of life in the early twentieth century. He asked me to make notes so that if his memory failed I would be able to remind him of his childhood, the town and people he knew so well and loved.

Other sources I have used are my father's diaries, photographs and letters which he wrote to his parents. The diaries date from 1912 and contain a mixture of entries relating to the family, friends, business, local, national and international events. It was typical of him that all photographs are carefully labelled and dated.

Father had a great affection for Chelmsford and, apart from the two years he spent in the army, he lived the whole of his eighty six years within a mile of Tindal Square. Born in the reign of Queen Victoria, he lived under five more monarchs and through two World Wars. I believe he saw more changes in the town and the lifestyle of its people than could ever have been envisaged in 1900.

PRUE JAMES

B H H and his parents. 1902

CHELMSFORD, THE COUNTY TOWN OF ESSEX

To set the scene for my childhood it is necessary to know a little about the County Town in the latter years of Queen Victoria's reign.

In 1877 Edmund Durrant, the Chelmsford bookseller, publisher, stationer and founder of the Chelmsford Odde Volumes, published a small book entitled *Durrant's Handbook of Essex*. This had been largely written by Miller Christy, an erudite historian and naturalist, the author of a number books on Essex. Miller Christy was justifiably proud of the town. "Chelmsford", he wrote, "is in all respects a model, well-built, clean, lively and orderly town - most certainly the handsomest in the county." It has to be said that this comment was in stark contrast to that of Charles Dickens who, when forced by torrential rain to spend a night in the Black Boy in 1834, is reputed to have labelled Chelmsford as "the dullest and the most stupid spot on the face of the earth".

The focal point, as it had no doubt been for several hundred years, was the parish church of St Mary the Virgin with its quaint spire. The area around St Mary's was full of life and activity. Small dwellings were clustered around the church, lining the narrow streets. Many of these houses had shops and businesses attached. New Street, High Street, Duke Street, Church Street, Threadneedle Street, Cottage Place and Legg Street pulsated with parochial life.

To the south of the parish church was the Square, where until 1879 the weekly cattle market was held. The Square had, until 1852, been known as Conduit Square but the conduit was then moved to the junction of Springfield Lane and the High Street and a statue of Judge Tindal erected in its place. Sir Nicholas Conyngham Tindal had been born and educated in Chelmsford and in 1829 had been appointed Lord Chief Justice of Common Pleas. The Square was naturally renamed Tindal Square and Conduit Street became Tindal Street.

There had been other recent changes in the town centre. In 1855 a cannon - a Russian 36 pounder - had been captured by the British at Sebastopol and subsequently presented to the town by Major Skinner. It was placed in front of the Shire Hall, where it remained for many years before being moved to Oaklands Park. The Corn Exchange dated from the 1850s when it was built to the design of Frederick Chancellor.

It is no wonder that the people of Chelmsford were proud of their town in the latter part of the nineteenth century. The town was compact and the community was closely-knit with, by the 1880s, a population of nearly ten thousand people. It was set in the midst of rich agricultural country and on market days its streets were thronged with farmers. The town had many fine inns which were full to bursting point as the local farmers celebrated their successful business deals or drowned their sorrows.

Up until the Great War the essential character of Chelmsford remained largely unaltered despite the increase in population and the advent of the Hoffman Manufacturing Company, the Marconi Wireless Telegraph Company and Colonel Crompton's Arc Works. It was to be many more years before much of our heritage would be tragically lost, with the seemingly wanton destruction of the Corn Exchange and Tindal Street.

This, then, was the environment into which I, the first child of a Duke Street grocer and his young wife, was born in the year 1900.

Chelmsford Cathedral

THE WORLD OF No. 9 DUKE STREET

It did not take many years to find out that I lived in the very centre of the universe! Not only was 9 Duke Street, Chelmsford, my home and my father's grocery shop, it was also the spot from which, turning in any direction, I saw sights both fascinating and exciting to a small boy born at the very beginning of the twentieth century.

If I looked out of the windows over the shop I was aware, in the street below, of the heavy horse-drawn trucks and carts making a tremendous noise on the irregular stone setts with their iron shod horses hooves and iron bound wheels. What a volume of traffic there was in both directions, coming to and going from the town centre, and always there seemed to be a Great Eastern Railway horse drawn truck, laden with heavy goods being delivered to the shops, and driven by Mr Esau Rich, the carrier. Looking out of the kitchen or scullery window I could not fail to be conscious of the massive pile of the Parish Church of St Mary the Virgin. If it were the right time of morning, and if it were sunny, I could not help but notice the great shadow sweeping up to the very house itself. I soon became familiar with the churchyard; it was my one and only playground for a number of years. There was no garden behind my home, only a narrow passage beyond which stood the churchyard wall. I was indeed fortunate in having good friends in the verger and the gardener. With their blessing I spent many happy hours bowling my hoop along the paths.

Standing on the front step of the shop and looking towards Tindal Square I soon learned that I was seeing the very centre of Chelmsford. There, in that open space, was a monument in stone of one of the famous men of Chelmsford - Judge Nicholas Tindal. There, too, was the Shire Hall as well as the Corn Exchange, a centre of great activity on Fridays.

As I looked across Duke Street from the shop step, I could see the narrow street named Threadneedle Street, and I knew that just around the corner was the Town Fire Station - an exciting place if ever there was one! I had been taken over to the Station several times by Percy Bragg, my father's assistant in the shop. At the sound of the fire horn Mr Bragg, if he could be spared from the shop for a few minutes, would hurry with me across Duke Street and down Threadneedle Street to watch the exciting drill of catching the horses and starting up the fire to work the pump. How thrilling it was to see the members of the Fire Brigade dashing up on foot or on bicycles and donning their uniforms on the fire engine as the galloping horses drew it away to the fire.

Percy Bragg worked for Father for many years and was just like one of the family. It was during my time in the army that Father wrote to tell me that Mr Bragg was leaving Chelmsford. I replied to my parents, "The old shop will never

Father standing outside shop shortly before demolition

seem the same without Mr Bragg. My mind goes back, and I can see myself dimly, being fed by him at breakfast when a baby and also having those glorious rides in the sugar tub in the top store room."

Only a stone's throw away was the comparatively modern cattle market, an up-to-date version of the centuries-old market which had previously stood in Tindal Square and the top of the High Street. One of the memorable pleasures of my young life was to be taken to the market by my maternal grandfather, Thomas Reynolds of Springfield, a retired farmer and butcher. I loved to walk up and down the rows of pens in the cattle market while grandfather weighed up the merits and the faults of the livestock awaiting the auction.

How fortunate I was to spend my childhood years in Duke Street. It was lined with shops from Tindal Square as far as the railway station and there were already quite a few more up to the corner of the Broomfield Road. I soon knew the whereabouts of the butcher and the fishmonger, the jeweller and the old clothes shop kept by Mrs Warner. Next door was a little eating house, run by Mr and Mrs Pinkenburg. Mr Pinkenburg had a strange, guttural accent which I found hard to understand. Old Mrs Ballard had an umbrella shop; she used to invite me into her house to help her make her bed! There were tailors, hatters, harness makers, fruiterers, a wine shop, two restaurants, a paper shop and a tobacconist where cigarettes were handmade in the window.

Possibly one of my greatest joys of all was to see the big double doors of the Golden Fleece unlocked and folded back as the church clock sounded opening time. The public bar was parallel with the pavement and every day I had the exquisite pleasure of seeing the landlord - Mr Barnaschina - gently pulling on one of the beer engines and slowly filling a glass tankard with the Gravesend Brewery's famous Shrimp Brand Bitter Beer. After holding it up to the light, Mr Barnaschina would raise it to his lips and decide whether or not it was up to his required standard. To pull those lovely wooden, china and brass beer engines was a consuming desire throughout my childhood, and even took precedence over my earlier ambition to drive a railway engine.

How I loved to stand on the shop doorstep and to watch the ever changing pictures of the various activities! What could have been more refreshing than to watch, on a hot August morning, the slow approach of the horse drawn water cart spraying water over the width of the dusty road and to feel a few drops on my bare legs. I remember, too, watching the German Boys' Band marching down the Duke Street. The band came to Chelmsford several years running and stayed the night at the Golden Fleece opposite - no doubt sleeping in the stables. At certain times throughout the day they assembled in a half circle on the pavement, wearing their stiff peaked caps and tight fitting tunics, and played patriotic German tunes to the delight of onlookers and passers-by.

Friday mornings were always special, as this was the day of the weekly cattle auction. Before describing the excitement which market day brought to the centre of the town, I should first explain that the two main front doors to my father's shop were on rising hinges and could be completely removed if so desired. Removal of the doors meant that the step into the shop was left free for the display of biscuits in glass lidded tins, and also a huge wooden cask filled with many varieties of Huntley and Palmer's broken biscuits.

On Fridays, however, the doors were never removed from their hinges. If it was a warm summer's day the doors might be folded back, but were always ready to be closed at a moment's notice. Why? The answer, of course, was connected with the market. In those days a large number of livestock was sent to Chelmsford market each week from all over the county and the bulk of it arrived in the town by train. Having been unloaded from the railway wagons, the animals were herded into the goods yard of the Great Eastern Railway in New Street. The responsibility of getting the livestock from the goods yard to the cattle market was in the hands of the drovers. I loved to watch these rough, unkempt men with their dogs - but I always watched from a safe distance!

So with deafening shouts from the drovers, the fierce barking of their dogs and the frightened cries of the animals the procession would set off on its half mile journey to the cattle market. The route was a direct one - along New Street and under the railway bridge, past Guy Harlings, Maynetrees and the side of the Shire Hall. Then into the top of the High Street from where they would move into Tindal Square and thence to Market Road by the side of the Corn Exchange. Passing Brittain Pash's store of agricultural implements they would enter the market where the animals would be penned in the appropriate enclosures. This apparently straightforward manoeuvre was what was supposed to happen, but how differently it often turned out in practice.

It was like a child's game played on a board with all kinds of hazards and pitfalls! There were so many other more tempting routes for the cattle to venture into if they had a chance. There was the turning into Victoria Road and Bradridge's Mill, there was Cottage Place by the Wheatsheaf, there was the open coach entry to the King William IV and the narrow Church Street by the Vestry Hall. If the cattle could be steered past all these, they then approached the biggest hazard of all - St Mary's Churchyard! The entrance in the extreme north-east corner of the churchyard wall revealed the soft, velvety lawns of the church-yard. Catching sight of the lush grass the whole company of bullocks, cows, pigs and sheep would hurl themselves at this narrow entrance to what must have appeared to them to be a veritable Garden of Eden. There were no fewer than seven ways out of the churchyard - ways of escape to the High Street, back to the railway yard, into Legg Street and into Tindal Square. But the route usually chosen, with drovers and dogs hot in pursuit, was the narrow opening of Cottage Place between No. 9 Duke Street and Walter Day's tailor's shop at No. 10.

This, then, was the reason why my father kept the shop doors in place on Fridays, and why, at the first suspicion of shouting across the churchyard, the doors were unceremoniously shut fast. Once the main mass of cattle had found its way across Duke Street, down Threadneedle Street and into the market the pandemonium subsided and the neighbourhood of the shop reverted to its customary life and movement.

The return journey of the cattle to the railway yard on their way to their new homes was generally much less exciting. By late afternoon most of the drovers were in a state of intoxication and their dogs were tired and hungry. It seemed that the cattle, left largely to their own devices, made their way back to the goods yard in New Street with no trouble at all.

Father and Percy Bragg outside shop in 1902

65 High Street, about 1890. Basil Henry Harrison and Alderman A G E Morton

GRANDFATHERS

My paternal grandfather, Basil Henry Harrison, had spent his early days in Kent, moving to Chelmsford in the late 1860s with his wife and two young sons.

Grandfather was an ironmonger by trade; he had a forge in Springfield Road opposite the Old Black Boy, and a shop on the west side of the High Street. The family, into which three more children were soon born, lived at first in New London Road and later over the shop at No. 65 High Street. This fine building, decorated along its elegant parapet with four stone ball finials, dated from about 1765 and had first belonged to Thomas Clapham, a hop merchant. Sadly, the building was demolished in 1972 and the present Marks and Spencer's was built on the site.

An old print of the High Street, published in 1863, shows that at that time the shop belonged to Mr Joseph Burton, a hat and cap manufacturer, merchant tailor, woollen draper and shirt maker. The main external feature of it was the large clock which extended over the pavement. The clock remained in place until Grandfather took over the upper floors of the building in the late 1870s. Father used to tell me how as a small boy he was fascinated by the boxed-in hole in the wall through which the clock had been wound in earlier days. The box had a little door through which he, his brothers and his sisters loved to stretch their hands and pretend that they were winding the clock.

By the time I was born in 1900 Grandfather and Grandmother had moved to Hamlet Road in Moulsham, and the upper storeys of 65 High Street were used solely for storage. My own treasured memories of the building are of the wonderful opportunities my cousins and I had for playing in the store rooms of the upper floors.

There was a wide staircase up to the former large reception rooms on the first floor, and less grand flights up to the bedrooms and attics. At the back of the house was the narrow servants' staircase down which we would clatter to the kitchen and from there to the outhouses. What games of hide-and-seek we enjoyed! I still remember the feeling of trembling anticipation as I crouched, huddled behind boxes, waiting to be pounced upon by one of my older cousins.

The outhouses, too, afforded all kinds of possibilities for children's fun and games. These small buildings, which were always incredibly dark and spooky, housed an enormous number of spiders, beetles and other creepy crawlies. There was no real garden, just a long and narrow yard with a brick built privy and a row of sheds which stretched towards New London Road. Looking back, I realise that many of the tools and the various preparations stored in these sheds must have been potentially dangerous to inquisitive small boys, but nobody seemed to worry unduly about us and we never came to any harm.

Tom and Ted Reynolds outside the shop on Springfield Hill

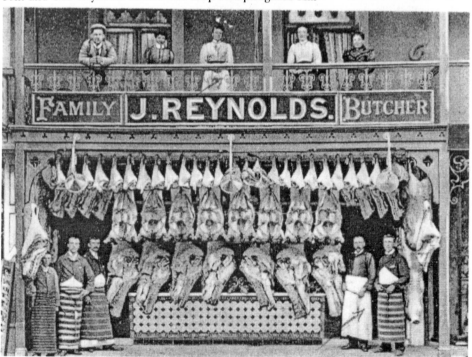

John Reynolds and his staff. Clara on balcony

My maternal grandfather was also a relative newcomer to Chelmsford. Thomas Reynolds had left his native Northamptonshire as a young man and had set up as a butcher in Plumstead, Kent. Following the premature death of his first wife he moved to Holders Farm at Springfield with his ten children. Within a few years he had sold the farm and moved to Elsie Villa in Arbour Lane, and this is where I remember him.

Elsie Villa was apparently designed by Grandfather's eldest son - a butcher, not an architect! As I cast my mind back over more than seventy years, I can remember the layout of the house with the utmost clarity and I feel that a more ill-planned house would be hard to conceive. There were awkward corners and odd steps everywhere and no two adjoining rooms were on the same level. I realise now that the house was of secondary importance; Grandfather's interest was wholly in the land. Here he had his smallholding which was also a part of his son's butchery business on Springfield Hill.

My mother was Grandfather's youngest child and was the only daughter who remained in the Chelmsford area after marriage. She visited her father and stepmother several times each week and as a small child I, of course, went with her. It was a pleasant walk from Duke Street to Arbour Lane. We would walk either through Tindal Square or across St Mary's churchyard to New Street and Waterloo Lane. In those days Waterloo Lane petered out at the bottom and we were then in Tunman Mead, a delightful area of watermeadows now the site of the Chelmsford Swimming Pool. It was just like being in the countryside and Father used to take a daily walk here. Taking care to keep away from the grazing cattle, we would follow the footpath until it emerged onto a rough track to the east of Regina Road. From there we had a choice of two routes.

Sometimes we would walk along the footpath, now known as the Bunny Walk, on the east bank of the River Chelmer. This was the route I preferred as not only were we right beside the water but also closer to the railway. I loved to see and hear the great steam engines rushing past on their way to the coast or to London. More often than not, however, we would make our way to Springfield Road and up the hill to call on Uncle Tom Reynolds.

Uncle Tom had a butcher's shop on Springfield Hill. He was a big, burly man with a luxuriant moustache and a neck as thick as those of his cattle. He looked in every way a butcher. I remember him as a kind and gentle man who always made us very welcome. Uncle Tom's shop was probably typical of butchers' shops in the early years of the twentieth century. In those days of far greater meat consumption than today and no refrigeration, butchers displayed huge quantities of meat at the front of their shops. Whole carcases hung close to the pavement, and the dust and flies which settled on them seemed to give no cause for concern.

Arbour Lane. In centre B H H, Mother and, in pram, brother

Reynolds grandparents

Often we took with us some groceries which Uncle Tom's wife, Aunt Annie, had asked for, and Mother chose a piece of meat for the next day or two. Letters and postcards were frequently sent between my parents and my uncle and aunt, recommending an especially fine joint of meat or a flavoursome piece of cheese. There seems to have been no problem with the postal delivery in those days - letters posted early in the morning would be delivered locally that day.

Uncle Tom's brother, John, was also a butcher. A picture postcard shows him with his assistants at the front of his shop surrounded by an impressive array of carcases. His wife, Clara, and other members of the family stand proudly on the balcony above. The message on the reverse offers Father (known in the family as 'Jack') a side of bacon and asks Father's opinion on John's own curing.

From Springfield Hill we made our way to Elsie Villa, by now carrying both groceries from Father's shop and meat from Uncle Tom's shop for Grandfather. On one occasion Frederick Spalding was in Arbour Lane, taking photographs. He asked Mother's permission for us to be in one of his pictures and there we still are, some eighty years later - Mother with my younger brother in his pram and I in my straw hat!

The smallholding was a paradise for me, especially because my own home in Duke Street had no garden - not even a back yard. The smallholding was a centre of great activity with pigsties, sheep pens, chicken houses and stables. There were high traps used for deliveries and a number of outhouses, both brick and wood. Best of all was an old railway carriage on concrete piers (to keep the rats and mice at bay) which was used for the storage of animal feed. Here I spent many happy hours with my Reynolds cousins as in our imagination we drove our 'train' all around the London Underground with the help of a map my cousin had somehow acquired. By the time I left school and went to work in the City I already knew every station of every line on the London Underground!

Every year there was the ritual of haymaking when Grandfather, my uncles, grown-up cousins and able-bodied volunteers would scythe the hayfield in one organised operation. Although I was still too young to be allowed to help I loved to watch the men at work, to smell the fresh hay and finally to see the haystack being built and thatched.

Grandfather was always busy outdoors - I rarely remember him inside his house. He used to wear a type of smock made from a coarse, unbleached material, possibly calico. Around his neck he always wore a red neckerchief. Tending his orchard, his vegetable and flower gardens filled his daylight hours until he died at Elsie Villa in his late eighties.

Basil Henry Harrison, 1840-1907   Victoria Hannah Harrison (née Ruck), 1839-1914

The new Wesleyan Church

THE WESLEYAN CHURCH

Both my mother's and father's families were staunch Wesleyans when I was young, and the Wesleyan Methodist Church by Chelmsford's Stone Bridge was our place of worship every Sunday. Although I was not of an age to appreciate the quality of the buildings, this was a fine new church, the funds for which had been raised by the unstinting efforts of the members. The previous church had been built in Springfield Road in 1843 but, in parallel with the population of the town, the number of members had increased to such an extent that it was necessary to build a larger church.

The site by the Stone Bridge was purchased at a cost of £1,350 in 1896 and although it occupied a prominent position in the town, there were problems to be overcome with regard to the foundations because of its proximity to the River Can. When completed the new church provided seating for more than seven hundred people, and the schoolroom accommodated another three hundred.

Grandfather, Basil Henry Harrison, was one of the trustees of the new church and his name was among those engraved on the west front of the building. I always felt proud to see his name there, especially as the inscription - 'B H Harrison' - also belonged to me, Basil Herbert Harrison!

The foundation stone of the church had been laid in June, 1897, and my parents' marriage in the summer of 1899 must have been among the first to be solemnised there. It was forty years later, after my mother's death, that I found a newspaper cutting from the *Essex County Chronicle* with a report on their wedding ceremony.

The bride's dress was described in detail and the report went on, "Her hat was of cream straw trimmed with silk and ospreys". I still chuckle to myself when I read those words and picture my mother walking up the aisle with those great birds of prey perched on her hat! The following year I was baptised there, and so began an association which was to last for the next twenty years.

The church was both a thriving centre of worship in Chelmsford and also provided a lively social life for its members. This was clearly necessary as there were still large debts to be paid for the building costs. The total cost of the project had amounted to £7,000 and to meet this there were church socials in winter, garden parties in summer, and frequent concerts and organ recitals. From my earliest days I can remember that my mother was always embroidering what she called 'fancy goods' for a forthcoming bazaar or sale of work.

Some of the garden parties were grand affairs, including the one held at Springfield Villa, the home of Mr George H Aubrey in July, 1902, just one week before my second birthday. I can be seen in the front row of the photograph, dressed in my finest white dress, white socks and little black shoes with ankle

The Wesleyan Bazaar in the Corn Exchange, 1905

straps. On my head is a frilly white hat, probably chosen as protection against the sun as well as being fashionable. The ladies' hats seem to vie with one another for the greatest number of feathers, flowers, fruit and other decorations!

Following the huge success of the Wesleyan Bazaar *Old Normandy* which was held in the Corn Exchange in 1898, it was decided to hold another large bazaar in 1905.

Mr G M Bridges of King's Lynn had been engaged in 1898 to provide scenery and stalls to add an authentic French touch, and many of the ladies had hired appropriate costumes from a theatrical supplier for the three day event. ⸳ The organisers continued with their policy of having a foreign country as their theme and for this occasion the title *Sunny Spain* was chosen. Although I was only five years old at the time of *Sunny Spain*, I can remember the atmosphere of excitement very clearly. I notice that in the photograph of the bazaar the ladies are once again dressed in national costume, the girls are beautifully dressed in white, the men are in their usual jackets and I am in my best sailor suit which I wore every Sunday. It amuses me now to think that, in those days when the Roman Catholic and Wesleyan churches were poles apart, the countries chosen as themes for the two bazaars were both predominantly Roman Catholic!

Every Sunday morning we attended church and my memories of it are mainly pleasurable. The old maxim still held good, that children should be seen and not heard, and it was no real hardship for me to sit quietly for an hour or so. From my earliest years I loved to sing, and I was always encouraged to join in with the hymns. Father had a fine bass voice and Grandfather, in his younger days, had been the leader of the choir. No doubt they hoped that I would carry on in the family tradition. I probably paid little attention to the spoken words of the service, unless they were aimed specifically at the children, but I can remember enjoying counting the windows, making up sums from the hymn numbers, trying to read anything I could see and generally keeping myself busy without fidgeting or speaking.

When the service finished Mother and Father always liked to talk to friends and relatives. I was fortunate in having one uncle and aunt who went out of their way to see that my cousins and I were not suffering from being surrounded by too many adults. Aunt Alice was a fine musician and was organist at the church. What could be better than joining her on the organ bench and being allowed to pull and push the stops at her request! Uncle Arthur was very much involved in the church and held several offices there. One of his duties was to count the collection after the morning service and, once I was old enough to be useful, he would take me with him to the vestry to help. I loved counting the coins and stacking them in neat piles; perhaps this was good training for my later years as a grocer.

HARRISON.—MR. B. H. HARRISON came to Chelmsford in 1866, and at once connected himself with the School. From 1874 to 1878 he was the leader of the Young Men's Class, and from 1878 to 1888 School Superintendent. For many years he taught the scholars their anniversary hymns. All the five children became teachers. Mr. A B. Harrison was for some time the School Organist and also trained the scholars. Mrs. A. B. Harrison taught and conducted the scholars the special hymns for 19 successive Anniversaries. Mr. H. J. Harrison was librarian and Mrs H. J. Harrison a teacher. Mr. W. H. Harrison was accepted as a teacher and collector in 1883. After a few years' absence he took up his duties again and in 1889 was elected as Secretary, which office he held until 1915, and served under five superintendents. Upon resigning the Secretaryship he was the recipient of a beautiful framed address as an expression of gratitude for his 26 years of faithful service. The following year he succeeded Mr. A. R. Morton as School Treasurer which position he held until the present year. Mrs. W. H. Harrison has been the absentee visitor for the past 13 years. Their three sons Messrs. Cyril, Wilfred and Hubert were all on the staff of teachers and the latter two were star registrars. Mr. Basil Harrison was Superintedent's Assistant and also a teacher. MR. WILFRED HARRISON is the founder of the " Felixstowe Children's Own."

Extract from *Chelmsford Wesleyan Methodist Sunday School Centenary: History & Souvenir 1821 to 1921*

The Wesleyan Garden Party at Springfield Villa, 1902

An amusing tale which father told me when I reached the age of discretion comes to my mind. One of my uncles had married a member of the Baptist church who had decided to support her husband and attend the Wesleyan church. There was, however, just one tradition she found hard to accept. My aunt was used to receiving the communion wine in an individual glass while seated in her pew. In the Wesleyan church the congregation drank from a common chalice. Aunt simply could not take to the idea of drinking from the chalice after other people so always made sure that she was first to the communion table. The minister evidently did not think much of this and decided to get the better of her. From time to time, he would start the distribution of the wine at the other end of the row! This must have been a real battle of wills, but not even my aunt could find a way to beat the minister in such a situation!

As in all churches, it was considered vital to enlist the help and interest of the younger members. By the time I was thirteen years old I was helping in the Sunday School and only a few years later became Assistant Superintendent. At seventeen and a half years I became a fully fledged Wesleyan Methodist. The church and its associated activities provided me with many good friends and plenty of social activities throughout my young days.

Church Membership Card

THE PEOPLE

It is not surprising that many of the people with whom I came into contact were tradesmen and their families. Life in the centre of Chelmsford, however, provided me with a wonderful opportunity to observe, if not to actually rub shoulders with, all classes of society.

Living in the larger houses in Duke Street, New Street and the High Street were ladies, such as Miss Baker and Miss Green, who seemed to me to wage endless war against children, especially non-conformist children! Hostilities were at their most grim when children were caught bowling their hoops and whipping their tops in St Mary's Churchyard. Such conduct was not to be tolerated!

The verger, Mr Oswick, and the gardener, 'Old David' were far more approachable. They would even let me help them when they mowed the churchyard lawns. One man pulled a rope in front of the mower while the other pushed and occasionally I was allowed to help with the pushing. What a joy this was to a small boy whose father had no grass to mow, especially if Miss Baker or Miss Green should happen to walk through the churchyard and see me! In the protective company of these two men I revelled in a sense of somewhat smug safety, thanks to their reassuring presence.

At Guy Harlings, next door to Miss Green's house, lived the Rector, the Revd. Canon Lake. With his black cassock blowing in the breeze he appeared larger than life and, even as a very small child, I was always aware of the great respect with which he was treated. The church organist, Frederick Frye, also lived nearby at St Mary's Lodge in Cottage Place. I had been into the church many times with my father and had heard the organ being played by Mr Frye. What a majestic sound that great instrument made; its chords seemed to roll down the nave and flow into the farthest corners of the huge building. I had already been taught that God was all-powerful but surely, I thought, that description must also apply to Mr Frye if he could produce such a volume of sound.

People from all walks of life made up the population of Duke Street in the early years of the twentieth century. From butchers to bootmakers, gardeners to grooms, mantle makers to medical practitioners and cutlers to confectioners, all lived and worked in Duke Street. All trades and professions were represented and added to the rich tapestry of domestic and business life.

The businesses were mainly small family concerns and were very different from the chain stores and faceless organisations which have now superseded them. Almost without exception the shopkeepers lived on the premises and it suited them well to do so. It was usual for shops to close for at least an hour in the middle of the day, but most of them opened early in the morning and closed late in the evening.

The customers who patronised my father's grocery shop came to him for several reasons. Many of them were tradespeople living in the neighbourhood of Duke Street and theirs was a 'tit for tat' arrangement. Some customers were members of the newly-built Wesleyan Methodist Chapel by the Stone Bridge where we worshipped every Sunday. Others came by way of my grandfather's recommendation.

Grandfather, Basil Henry Harrison, had a wholesale and retail ironmongery business in the High Street. There was a great feeling of loyalty between tradesmen and customers. The customers gave the shops their loyal support and the shopkeepers served the customers with courtesy and consideration.

Should the weather be unpropitious, the Procession and open-air Service will not take place, the Afternoon Fête will be carried out as far as possible, and the Children's Tea will be in the Drill Hall, while the Ball will begin at 9 p.m. instead of 10.45.

The Bowling Greens will be open for Bowls all day, and the general public are requested not to walk upon the greens, or upon the flower beds, or upon the grass near the river.

The New Courts near the Railway Arches will be open for lawn tennis.

Tradesmen are invited to decorate their business premises, and inhabitants their houses.

For lost children or any information apply at the Honorary Secretary's Office and Police Head-Quarters, near the Band Stand.

God Save the King !

J. O. THOMPSON,

Hon. Secretary.

.dvertisement in Coronation programme, 1911

SATURDAYS

Saturday was always an exceptionally busy day for Father and, doubtless, for all the shopkeepers in the centre of town. While Friday's customers were largely from the rural areas around Chelmsford, Saturday's trade was almost entirely devoted to those who lived within a stone's throw of our shop. Many of these loyal followers of Father had no option but to do their weekly shopping on Saturday for the simple reason that it was not until Friday teatime that the workmen were paid for their week's labours.

A small number of people did their shopping as soon as they had received their money on a Friday, but the great majority preferred to wait until the following day. On Saturdays Father opened his shop from 7 in the morning until 9 o'clock in the evening. Business was very brisk in the early morning and then tended to ease off slightly towards dinner time. The afternoon and evening brought more customers and the whole town was thronged with people.

Quite apart from the hustle and bustle inside the shop, the centre of the town was so exciting to a small boy aged between six and ten years. Enjoying my freedom from school on a Saturday, I loved to walk alone down Duke Street, through Tindal Square and along the High Street. This was a privilege for daylight hours only, and I was constantly reminded that I was allowed no further than the Queen's Head. This did not present any real restriction as there was so much of interest in my permitted area.

There was never any question of getting into serious mischief. I would almost certainly have been noticed and word would have got back to my parents via relatives, neighbours or fellow Wesleyans. Uncle Arthur's printing shop was on the corner of Market Road and Tindal Square, near the Golden Lion, and Grandfather's ironmongery business was on the west side of the High Street. Thus I was almost sure to be spotted!

It was not, however, always necessary to go outside to find entertainment. The upstairs windows of the back of our home afforded a superb bird's eye view of the many marriages which were solemnised at the Parish Church of St Mary. Perched at the windowsill, I was in the perfect position to watch the activities of the bridal parties clustered around the south porch of the church. I remember well the ornate and enormous hats worn by the ladies and the flowing white dresses of the brides. But for a small boy the best was yet to come! It was almost certain that later in the afternoon the happy couple would leave by train for their honeymoon. Then there would be such a thrilling and penetrating sound as the engine driver, having received some suitable 'pourbois' from the best man, would sound the steam whistle. As soon as the train started to draw out of the station the shrill joyful bursts from the whistle would be heard all over the town until at last the train disappeared under either the bridge at Widford or at Arbour Lane in Springfield.

Many happy incidents and routines connected with Saturday afternoons flash across my mind. I think in particular of our neighbour across the road. This was Mrs Coney, wife of the harness maker. The Coneys lived in the house directly to the east of the Golden Fleece. Every Saturday afternoon Mrs Coney spent a considerable time sweeping and scrubbing not only the doorstep and front of the shop, but also the pavement. Having at last completed her work she would fetch two little wooden chairs and place them on either side of the door. Her two young daughters would then emerge from inside the shop and would sit in solemn state watching the traffic and the passers by. Perhaps their presence was meant to deter people from treading on the freshly washed pavement? I shall never know, but I shall always remember the Coneys.

If I was lucky I might be taken out by Mother or Father after tea on a Saturday, especially if the season happened to be late autumn with Christmas not so far away. The main streets, including Duke Street, were lit by electric standard lamps using the most modern methods of illumination developed by Colonel Crompton at his factory in Lower Anchor Street. A familiar sight was that of workmen on a high gantry-like erection on wheels moving from lamp to lamp renewing the black carbon rods and testing the mechanism, necessary to regulate the distance between the rods through which the current flowed.

Walking down Duke Street into Tindal Square I would become increasingly aware of music and in a few moments would see the local Salvation Army Silver Band providing the music for their Saturday evening service. This was always held by the Sebastopol cannon in front of the Shire Hall and the band would stand in a semi-circular formation with the remaining Salvationists around them. Passers-by and those who stopped to listen or to join in with the hymns filled the adjacent pavements and overflowed onto the road. This area was always a bottleneck early on a Saturday evening and the traffic had to make slow, cautious progress from Tindal Square into the High Street.

But the Salvation Army Band was not the only attraction!. It occasionally happened that the bells of St Mary's Church - a mere couple of hundred yards from the Shire Hall - would be rung on a Saturday evening. What a cacophony of sound was produced by the church bells and the Salvationists making music at such close quarters! For some people the sound of the bells was never anything more than an unmitigated nuisance while for others the sounds were joyful and sweet. I, born in the shadow of the bell tower, have always loved the pealing, cascading sound.

In Tindal Square and the High Street the paper boys, each eager to do more trade than the others, shouted the news at the tops of their voices, while outside the Queen's Head the red-faced man on the shellfish stall encouraged everyone within a hundred yards or so to buy his cockles, mussels and winkles. On the corner of Barrack Square the brazier of the baked potato and roasted chestnut stall glowed brightly - the deliciously appetizing smell is one I will never forget. Potatoes and chestnuts were more to our taste than shellfish and even now, some eighty years later, my mouth waters at the memory of them.

As Saturday evening advanced so the noise increased. What else could one expect when it is remembered that between our shop and London Road corner, via Tindal Street, there were the following pubs - the Golden Fleece, Golden Lion, Bell Hotel, Market House, White Hart, Spotted Dog, Dolphin and (until 1906) the Half Moon. Eight pubs in a few hundred yards, and others in the High Street. Is it any surprise to know that Mr Turner, a well known Chelmsford evangelist given to proclaiming the Gospel in Tindal Square, ended the evening immersed in the horse trough on more than one occasion!

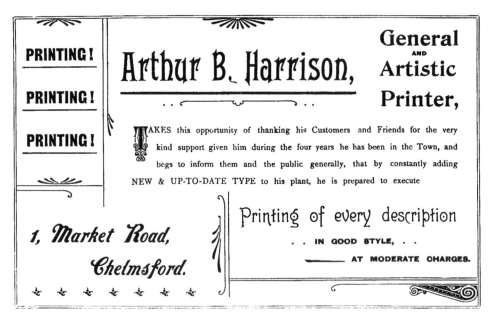

Arthur Harrison's advertisement in the *Official Handbook* of the Grand Bazaar, 1898

TWO DISTURBED NIGHTS IN DUKE STREET

I was five years old when there was an incident in the town centre which brought many of the residents from their beds. A reverberating explosion shattered the peace and quiet of the foggy night and many people, including my father, hurried outside into the streets to see what had happened. The cause of the deafening sound was immediately clear, as smoke could be seen still coming from the muzzle of the cannon. This was the cannon which had been captured from the Russians during the Crimean War and had stood for half a century outside the Shire Hall. Several policemen, alerted by the cannon's roar, were soon on the scene and found that a canister of gunpowder with a fuse attached must have been placed in the mouth of the gun. Later, fragments of the canister were found scattered across Tindal Square. Nobody ever knew for certain who the culprits were, but many had a good idea of the identity of the ringleader. The practical jokers had undoubtedly waited until the sound of any policemen's footsteps had died away before lighting the fuse. In the general confusion that followed they were able to escape quietly from the scene into the fog.

Although I can still remember the echoes of the explosion and being tucked, half asleep, into my parents' bed with my mother, I have no recollection of my father's return. No doubt I was fast asleep! Soon afterwards the barrel of the cannon was sealed with a stout wooden plug and more than thirty years later, in 1937, the Russian trophy was moved to Oaklands Park.

In 1930 the *Essex Weekly News* refreshed its readers' memories by writing about the incident in its feature, "Men and Memories of Twenty-Five Years Ago".

It must have been just a couple of years later that we owed a debt of gratitude to our neighbour Mrs Coney, the wife of the saddler and harness maker. One hot July night she was unable to sleep and went downstairs to get some air in the doorway. As she stood, gratefully breathing in the fresh night air, she was alarmed to see smoke billowing out from the gratings in front of our shop. Rushing across the road in her night attire she hammered on the door and rang the bell until Father was at last awakened by the noise.

He was then immediately conscious of the smell of burning and rushed down to the basement. On opening the heavy, windowed doors to the area he found there was an accumulation of rubbish, which should have been cleared away, already well alight.

The fire had probably been started by a cigarette end dropped through the grating in the pavement and the flames were already beginning to lick the paint on the woodwork of the doors. Fortunately, water was readily at hand in the adjoining scullery in the basement and, with the help of a passing policeman, danger was soon averted.

I can just remember being awakened in my bedroom at the back of the house by my mother, who carried me downstairs in my nightshirt and stood near the door with me until the danger had passed. We were soon able to go back to bed but I doubt whether sleep returned as easily to Father and Mother as to me. I imagine that before they slept they expressed their thanks to God for their fortunate escape from a blaze which could have been disastrous had it not been for the timely vigilance of our good neighbour.

The Sebastopol Cannon

FATHER'S APPRENTICESHIP AND BEYOND

As I 'helped' Father in the shop when I was a young schoolboy, I loved to hear him talk of his own youth and of his entry into the grocery trade. He had, I believe, always taken it for granted that he would spend his working life in a shop, and had always hoped that one day he would have his own business.

My father was educated at King Edward VI Grammar School, then situated in Duke Street where County Hall now stands. I am not sure how old he was when he left school, but he worked for at least a couple of years in his father's ironmongery business. Then, like his two older brothers, he served an apprenticeship. His oldest brother, Arthur, had been apprenticed to a bookseller and printer in Haverfordwest in Pembrokeshire. Why, I often wonder, was he sent so far from home? The next brother, Walter, had served his apprenticeship in ironmongery and had later taken over his father's business in the High Street.

Father had the good fortune to be apprenticed locally to Mr Walter Fortin Catt, who had a flourishing grocery business on the south side of Tindal Square. His apprenticeship began on the first day of August, 1888, and he received an extremely thorough training during his three years with Mr Catt. Father always looked back on those years with pleasure and felt that they stood him in good stead for his years in the grocery trade.

Many of the tasks allotted to Father were physically much harder than those of today's grocery or supermarket assistant. His duties as an apprentice included sawing lump sugar and lump salt into manageable chunks. He had to literally dig the coarse Barbados sugar from the enormous hogsheads in which it was imported into this country. Currants, sultanas and raisins arrived in a solid mass, matted together with stalks, stones and all manner of identifiable and unidentifiable foreign bodies. All these commodities had then to be packaged and weighed for the customers. Soap, too, had to be cut and was sold by weight, and there were a hundred and one other jobs which were always given to the apprentice. Father received thorough training in handling provisions. He could bone a side of bacon with great skill, and could cut back rashers by hand as evenly as the machine which he was to buy some thirty years later. The hours were lengthy, and it was often late in the evening by the time he returned with the horse and cart from the delivery round.

Evidently Father's work gave satisfaction. His indentures are endorsed "Served satisfactorily" and are signed "W F Catt". Five years later, having gained further valuable experience with an employer in Kent, he was set up in business in Duke Street through the generosity of his father and an uncle.

The row of six three-storey brick houses, each with a cellar, had been built at the very end of the eighteenth century. No. 9 was the most westerly of these

Settlement of Transfer of Business and Effects at 9 Duke Street
Chelmsford

Mr. H. J. Harrison   in account with   Mr. M. Strange

Nov 20th 1896

Dr.	£	s.	d.		Cr.	£	s.	d.
Lease and Goodwill	150				Deposit	25	"	"
Fixtures and Utensils in Trade					Rent to Date	5	10	4
Tenant's House Fixtures					Assessed Taxes — House Duty		3	9
Furniture					Parish Rates } to be settled hereafter by the parties			
Horses and Carts					Water Rate }			
Stock in Trade	432	10	7		Gas	273		
Proportion of Licenses		3	6		Cheque or Cash	139	18	1
" Parish Rates					Bill or Note at 2 months		9	7
" Insurance		10	.		Ditto ditto 3	140	9	7
Interest on Bills	2	17	8		Balance			
	£586	1	9			£586	1	9

Messrs. COOK & SMITH,
Trade Valuers, Accountants and Auctioneers,
47 & 48, King William Street, London Bridge, E.C.

2·10·7   Appraisers Award
         Strange to Harrison
                November 20th 1896

We the undersigned having appraised the Stock
in trade of Grocery, Provisions, Brushes, Brooms
Drapatery etc etc of and from Matthew Strange of
9 Duke Street, Chelmsford, to John Herbert Harrison
of Hamlet Road, Moulsham.
We declare the value to be Four Hundred and Thirty
two pounds Ten Shillings and Seven-pence
£432.10.7 —————————————————
Fixtures Fittings and Utensils as per agree c
one Hundred and Fifty pounds
£150 —

                    Charles Heathly
                    18 Springfield Rd
                    Chelmsford
         and   Cook Smith

              Auctioneers Valuers & Accountants
              47 + 48 King William Street
                    London Bridge EC

Appraiser's Award, 1896

31

and was already used as a grocer's shop by Mr Matthew Strange. Grandfather and Uncle John Sankey bought the business premises, for which Father paid them rent, and also the stock including brushes, brooms and drysaltery.

Prior to Mr Strange's ownership the building had apparently been used by a pawnbroker. As a child I was intrigued and somewhat scared by a side door which was firmly fastened and never opened. Father later told me that it was used by self-conscious townsfolk who preferred this less noticeable entrance when they needed to slip in to 'Uncle's for a bit of ready cash!

In 1896, just four years before my birth, 9 Duke Street opened for trading under the name of H J Harrison, Private Grocer and Provision Merchant. How fortunate Father was to be in such a good location - a busy street close to the town centre, packed tightly with shops and inns above almost all of which lived families. It may seem strange that Father's business was situated so close to that of his former employer, Mr Walter Catt of Tindal Square. This, in fact, caused no problem or embarrassment as each grocer catered for a different clientèle. Mr Catt was a member of St Mary's Church, while Father was a Wesleyan. Both were supported by their fellow worshippers. Mr Catt held a Gilbey licence for the sale of wines and spirits while Father - a lifelong teetotaller - would have never considered selling alcohol.

Matthew Strange had, apparently, sold more tobacco than groceries in his last years of business. Most of his customers had come from the smaller homes in Cottage Place, Legg Street and New Street. Father decided right from the start that he would not sell tobacco, but would concentrate instead on building up the grocery trade. He had his eye on the larger and more prosperous catchment area of the whole length of Duke Street, where the only other grocery shop was Martin's at the corner of Broomfield Road.

Father's first Pass Book for the London and County Banking Co. Ltd. includes the names of companies which are still well-known to-day - Cadbury, Fry, Lever, Bovril, Crosse, Bird, Huntley, Rowntree and Reckitt. How comforting it is, in this era of change, to know that some things are the same as in my childhood.

It soon became clear, however, that Father needed to specialise in one particular commodity and, looking around, he found that no other Chelmsford grocer sold fresh coffee. Coffee beans, or berries as they are known in the trade, soon become stale and lose their flavour and aroma once they have been roasted. The coffee sold in most shops at that time bore no reference to its country of origin and there was, in general, little interest in it. The journey of coffee from the plant to the cup was a long one.

Having been brought by ship from such distant parts as Africa, South America and Jamaica, it was stacked in bonded warehouses until sold in the

Coffee Sale Room in London's Mincing Lane to coffee wholesalers. Much of it received no expert blending before being roasted, ground and finally despatched with other goods to the shops. There it was usually stored in a biscuit tin under the counter and not infrequently mixed up with the stale remains of the last delivery.

It must have been an exciting day for Father when, with advice from his coffee supplier Walter Willams and Co. of London, he bought the necessary equipment for his new venture. I remember the large coffee canisters clearly - they were so gay with their Oriental design and colouring and must have attracted much attention when they first appeared in the window. Even after all these years I can almost feel their shining smoothness and see the intricate pictures of exotic birds and flowers on the glossy red background. There was also a beautiful mahogany and brass balance, a couple of attractive brass scoops and half a dozen brightly decorated shallow papier mâché bowls.

White paper was used for wrapping and was bought in three sizes for quarter, half and one pound quantities. This paper had bold printing showing Father's name and address on the back, and there was suitably fine white string for tying up the packets. This was a task which needed some degree of manual dexterity. Every grain of coffee sold was flat wrapped and neatly tied. Finally there was a sticky label which showed the country of origin and also whether the contents were pure coffee or a mixture of coffee and chicory.

None of this equipment would have been of any use, however, without the all-important coffee grinder. This expensive item was bought second-hand and was a massive cast-iron grinder, extremely heavy and cumbersome. It had a large flywheel on one side to give the necessary momentum and on the other side, behind the counter, was a smaller wheel with a wooden handle. This smaller wheel had to be turned manually to grind the roasted berries into various grades of powder. The machine was not unlike those heavy, clumsy grinders used by farmers to break up food for cattle. It was a laborious job supplying the power for the grinder, but one which I learned to master as a comparatively small boy. I was willing to try my hand at almost anything if Father would reward me for my efforts with three or four chocolate drops!

One final item was needed for Father to launch his coffee drive - a bold notice to attract his regular customers and also passers-by. Mr Hall, the sign writer, provided this, and the meticulously written notice was placed in the window, stating in the clearest terms that the coffee for sale had been freshly roasted in the City of London that very morning.

It was a proud day for my father, on that Monday morning near the end of the long reign of Queen Victoria, when he raised the heavy dark blue roller blind and revealed for the first time a whole window devoted to coffee. What an achievement for those days! To obtain fresh coffee daily Father would send a telegram (twelve words for sixpence) to Walter Williams and Co. at their warehouse in a narrow courtyard just by the Aldgate Pump.

On receipt of these instructions the required quantity of berries would be roasted, packed while still warm and taken along to Liverpool Street Station. There the coffee would be put on a passenger train and collected at Chelmsford Station by the full-time errand boy. Father always preferred to order his coffee daily, believing that this was the best way to ensure that it was really fresh. The shop window, with its display of bowls filled with coffee berries and ground coffee, together with Mr Hall's notice attracted many new customers and Father's status as a Chelmsford grocer was established.

Despite the success of the coffee, business was inevitably difficult at times. In 1901 Father became seriously ill and was admitted to King's College Hospital in London. The hospital régime was very strict at that time and my mother's visits to London to see her sick husband must have been a time of great anxiety. My parents kept the letter of admission, on the back of which they were reminded that "Patients and Visitors to the Hospital must Strictly Observe the Following Rules". The following were typical,

"Visitors must not loiter on the staircases or passages of the Hospital, and when they have quitted the Ward, cannot be allowed to return on the same day."

"Visitors are not to sit on the beds; and they are not to touch any bottles, papers, boxes, or other articles in the Ward."

My poor mother had not only to look after me and to visit my father but also to put in a considerable amount of time in the shop. The staff at that time consisted of my father's assistant Percy Bragg, who was worth his weight in gold, and the errand boy.

Fortunately, Father's brother Walter came to the rescue to take charge of the financial side of the business until Father was well again. After that, life settled down into the stable period to which many of my most vivid memories belong.

The beginning of the Great War in August, 1914, was the point in history at which not only Europe, but the whole world, changed almost overnight. The wealth of mankind was to be squandered on destruction and Chelmsford, in keeping with every other place, changed rapidly. There was not a family in the country that was not affected and disrupted in a way which could never have been envisaged. Looking back, I am so thankful that I was old enough to have memories that stretched back to the apparently halcyon days before the grim horror and deprivation of that period.

It must be remembered that in those days there was no cut-throat competition from greedy giant combines, and business depended largely on the band of loyal customers who stuck to their chosen tradesmen through thick and

PATIENTS AND VISITORS TO THE HOSPITAL MUST STRICTLY OBSERVE THE FOLLOWING RULES.

THE VISITING DAYS are: Wednesdays, from Five to Six p.m.; Sundays and Christmas Day, Two to Four p.m.

Visitors on these Days will be admitted to the Ward in which their friends are staying, if clean and sober. They must conduct themselves in a quiet orderly manner whilst there. Not more than three friends in one day may visit a patient; and only two at a time may enter the ward. Children under eight years of age must not be brought to the Hospital, unless the mother or father be a Patient.

Visitors must not loiter on the staircases or passages of the Hospital, and when they have quitted the Ward, cannot be allowed to return on the same day.

Visitors must not go to the bed of any other Patient than that occupied by their own friend, nor into any other Ward.

Visitors are not to sit on the beds; and they are not to touch any bottles, papers, boxes, or other articles in the Ward.

Tea or Cocoa, Sugar and Butter, may be bought for the Patient's use, but no fruit of any kind must be given to any Patient except through the Sister of the Ward, who will obtain the approval of the proper Medical Officer for its use.

Wine, Beer, and Spirits are forbidden to be brought into the Hospital by any Patient or Visitor.

THE COMMITTEE have directed that any person breaking the above Rules shall be excluded from the Hospital.

It is the earnest desire of the COMMITTEE that all Patients in the Wards of the Hospital shall enjoy the greatest comfort and quiet in order that they may have the full benefit of the medical and surgical treatment, and of the nursing provided within the Hospital. It is necessary for this purpose that the above Rules be strictly observed.

By order of the Committee of Management,

N. BROMLEY, (REV.);

Warden.

KING'S COLLEGE HOSPITAL,

LINCOLN'S INN FIELDS,

.... 11/3/01 19

~~In reply to your enquiries,~~ I beg to inform

you that .... ~~for whom you desire admission as~~ an In-Patient, can be

received into the Hospital **on Wednesday**
next — the 13th inst —

provided the Medical authorities here deem ~~it~~ **you**, after

examination, a fit case for treatment as an In-Patient.

I am, *F. C. Carle*
House Surgeon.

To ...... *H. G. Harrison .*

THE Patient should attend for examination at One o'clock.

•••••••••••••••

Articles to be provided by friends of Patients on admission :—

Breakfast

~~CUP AND SAUCER.~~

★ PINT MUG.

★ KNIFE & FORK.

★ SPOON.

★ PLATE (small).

★ MILK JUG (small).

BRUSH AND COMB (tooth).

TOWELS.

SOAP.

TEA

SUGAR } ~~if required.~~

BUTTER

★ A CHANGE OF LINEN.

....

The Rules for Patients and Visitors will be found on the other side.

Portmanteaus and Boxes cannot be received.

Washing to be done by friends or paid for by the Patients.

★ These articles are not required for children under nine years of age.

36

Percy Bragg and George Skippen, assistants in the shop

thin. There was, however, always a number of customers who patronized several shops, perhaps coming to Father only for coffee. It was at the beginning of the Great War in 1914 and with the imminent threat of food shortages that Father found that many of his occasional customers wished to register with him for the provision of rationed commodities. So it was that in an unexpected way the war actually helped the business to expand, and Father and Percy Bragg had as much as they could do to cope with the extra trade.

This does not mean that life was easy for my father during this period. There were many problems with which he had to contend. Rationing and the extra documentation it necessitated was an added task, but by this time I was able to take over some of the paperwork after school hours.

Nearly seventy years later I still have a bar of soap from my father's shop. It was one of a number sold as a souvenir of the war, and is a model of Lord Kitchener, who was drowned at sea on 6th June, 1916. The soap was made by Margerison and Co. and sold at sixpence a bar. Lord Kitchener, with his long solemn face and his moustache looks gravely at me still. Once the soap was a creamy white colour, now it is parchment yellow, but it is a fine reminder of those days.

Essential commodities became more and more scarce and coffee - a peacetime luxury - was hard to come by. Father's policy of remaining loyal to one supplier paid dividends, and Walter Williams and Co. sent along whatever coffee they were able to obtain. This meant that from time to time regular customers were able to buy a small amount of fresh coffee. What a welcome stimulant it must have been in the dark days of the Great War.

IF FOUND, RETURN TO ANY FOOD OFFICE.

MINISTRY OF FOOD. Serial No. 2C N° 157804

NATIONAL RATION BOOK (B).

INSTRUCTIONS. [Read carefully.

1. The person named as the holder of this Ration Book on the Reference Leaf (page 6) (Green) must sign his name in the space provided on that leaf, and must copy in the space provided for it on the Reference Leaf the Serial Number appearing at the head of this cover.

2. The Book must be registered at once for the purchase of Sugar, Fats (i.e. **Butter, Margarine and Lard), Butcher's Meat and Bacon.** To register for Sugar the holder must sign his name and enter his address and date of signing on the Sugar Counterfoil (Yellow), and take the book to the sugar retailer. The retailer will enter his name and address in the proper space (numbered 1) on the inside of the cover and on the back of the counterfoil, and will detach and keep the counterfoil. Registration for other foods will be effected in the same way, by use of the counterfoils for Fats (Blue), Butcher's Meat (Red), and Bacon (Red).

3. Persons living in hotels, boarding houses, hostels, schools and similar establishments should not register their Ration Books until they leave the establishment.

4. The Ration Book may be used only by or on behalf of the holder, to buy rationed food for him or members of the same household or guests sharing common meals. It may not be used to obtain rationed food for others.

5. The Ration Book may only be used while the holder is living in Great Britain, is not drawing Government rations, and is not in an institution (hospital, asylum, workhouse, &c.). If he dies or joins the forces, or enters an institution, the book must be given up to the proper authority, that is to say, the Registrar of Deaths, the naval, military or air force authority, or the head of the institution, as the case may be. If the holder is leaving Great Britain for a period exceeding four weeks the book must

N.2.

Mr. J. HARRISON.

Continued on back cover.

38

ANNUAL EVENTS

Before I was very old I became aware that there was an annual pattern to my life and also to that of the town. Each season brought its own particular pleasures to be sampled and savoured.

Fairs were held twice yearly, in May and November, in the Bell Meadow. These were basically cattle fairs, but it was the attraction of a fair such as we know it today which drew me to these exciting events. The Bell Meadow was approached either from Tindal Street and through the Bell Hotel Yard, or from Threadneedle Street by the side of the Fire Station. Although I was never allowed to go inside the field on my own when the fair was in progress, it was possible to stand on the path of the Recreation Ground and see some of the activities. From there I had a close-up view of the steam roundabout with the wonderful mechanical organ complete with moving figures.

When fortune smiled on me, Mother and Father would take me to the Fair for a treat. What a stir of excitement there was as darkness fell and the brilliant electric lights came on, shining in all colours of the rainbow! Then the roundabout, hoopla stalls, coconut shies, boxing booth and swings were all transformed by the light supplied by the great dynamo, activated by the magnificent steam engine with its shining wheel.

Summertime brought picnics in the Rec (the local name for the Recreation Ground) and in Tunman Mead, where I picked huge bunches of the golden yellow buttercups during the long sunny afternoons. The water sparkled in the summer sunshine and I feel as though it was warm and sunny every day.

We were sufficiently fortunate to have an annual seaside holiday and usually travelled by train to Felixstowe. The *Felixstowe Visitors' List* for Saturday, 11th July, 1903, a supplement to the *East Anglian Daily Times*, shows that we were staying in Ranelagh Road for our holiday. Every adult visitor's name was listed in this publication.

Perhaps the high spot of the summer was the visit to Chelmsford of one of the great travelling circuses. The name which I remember spelling out with the utmost care and concentration was that of Lord George Sanger. This visit always created great excitement in the town, especially as the first performance was preceded by a thrilling procession through the centre of Chelmsford. The shop doorstep was not considered by my parents to be a safe spot for their small son to stand on this occasion, but the first floor windows above the shop were in just the right position for an excellent view of the whole proceedings. Here I was at the perfect height to see everything with the utmost clarity. And what wonderful sights I saw as I stood with my nose pressed against the window pane!

The noise in Duke Street grew steadily louder as the circus procession approached from the railway station, until at last it could be seen passing Webber's shop. It was indeed a tremendous thrill to see the huge grey elephants and, looking back after many years, it seems a sound idea to have them at the head of the procession because they set a stately, steady pace for the other performers to follow. After the elephants came a mixed collection of mounted cowboys, Red Indians, little Shetland ponies and what seemed like crowds of clowns and funny men. Then into sight came the first of several great lumbering wagons, brilliantly painted in gold and scarlet. The wagon was drawn by four powerful horses and driven by a coachman, resplendent in uniform and peaked hat with plenty of gold braid. In the wagon was the band, also smartly attired and making a great deal of sound on their shining brass instruments and drums. It may have been noise, rather than music, but I thought it was wonderful.

Behind the band came several similar wagons, but these were cages with thick iron bars containing fierce, wild animals. Even then, at my young age, I remember shivering with pleasurable terror at the sight of those lions and tigers.

Then came the climax of the procession. This was a wagon built up rather like a gold and red two-tiered cake on top of which sat Britannia, dressed in a golden breastplate and helmet to match, with her trident in one hand and her shield in the other. Oh! What a wonderful sight she was! This great lumbering wagon drawn by four - or perhaps it was six - smart horses was to youthful eyes the very essence of perfection.

Nothing could better this display of England's might, and indeed nothing did surpass it for the simple reason that Britannia was always at the end of the circus procession, except for the usual stable boys and various hangers-on.

As the procession moved out of Duke Street, through Tindal Square and down the High Street the noise would decrease, my father would resume his normal work and customers would once again come into the shop. The procession would turn up Springfield Road from the High Street and then move through the narrow opening by my grandfather's forge into the King's Head Meadow. The Meadow would be a hive of activity as the circus finally arrived and the Big Top, which had been erected earlier in the day, would dominate its surroundings in readiness for the evening performance.

The atmosphere was charged with hustle, bustle and excitement. I was, however, never taken to a circus performance when I was young. Looking back over the years, I suppose I was unaware of what I was missing, but I do not recall any desire to see the animals and clowns performing. After all, I had watched the whole procession from start to finish from my vantage point above the street and, surely, nothing could be more exciting!

The Corn Exchange was the scene of a variety of events and was in great demand throughout the year. Spread over the twelve months we saw the arrival and departure of many entertainers. There were travelling theatre companies, concerts by local artistes, lantern lectures and trade exhibitions. It was at one of these trade exhibitions that I was photographed at the age of six.

Once a year word spread on the small boys' bush telegraph of the arrival of Poole's Mirrorama - a most ingenious form of moving spectacle. Huge circular drums were painted with various exciting historical incidents such as the Retreat from Moscow, the Battle of Waterloo, the Battle of Trafalgar and General Gordon's death at Khartoum.

We boys used to crowd around the open side door of the Corn Exchange and watch the 'trial run' as the great drums slowly revolved and revealed their vast, moving spectacle. In those days before television brought visual entertainment right into our homes, we would stand glued to the spot and completely spellbound. Almost as exciting was when, in the darkness of the evening, the door was kept firmly closed and we were thus denied even the briefest glimpse of the delights inside the Corn Exchange. We could only stand outside, listening to the voice of the narrator, the music of the band and the martial sounds of bugles and gunfire. And all the time we could hear those great drums revolving at their various speeds and positions on the stage, revealing to the audience those epic events of history unfolding before their eyes.

There was always plenty to do and lots to look forward to. In common with most children of that period my friends and I were able to amuse ourselves without being a nuisance to others. Our pastimes were, on the whole, the result of imagination and initiative. They cost nothing and left me free to squander my weekly ha'penny on sweets.

B H H and parents on holiday in 1902. Probably Felixstowe

WALKING BLINDFOLD FROM BROOMFIELD ROAD TO MOULSHAM STREET

I am sure that I could have found my way blindfold from end to end of the town simply by using my nose! From Broomfield Road corner, where the real countryside began, I would walk down Duke Street towards the centre of Chelmsford. Even in those days before refrigeration there was only the slightest awareness of Mr Pannell's shop and I appreciate now just how fresh the fish must have been. A few seconds later I would catch the appetizing smell of fresh bread from Mr Shedd's bakery. Had I uncovered my eyes I would have seen a delicious assortment of bread and cakes in the window.

Soon afterwards, on my right was the timber yard of Messrs. Wells and Perry (where the bus station now stands), with its unmistakable redolence of newly sawn timber. Then there was the acrid smoky smell of the railway station; sometimes just a slight whiff, but at other times the air would be thick with smoke and smuts. Beyond the station I soon reached Hawkes sweet shop with its deliciously tempting and sugary smell. Oh, those gob-stoppers and toffees - I can taste them still! The Chelmsford Brewery came next and with it the wonderful heady aroma of hops. This brewery, also owned by Wells and Perry, stood between the corner of Victoria Road and the Lion and Lamb.

And so down the Duke Street, passing on my way a variety of small shops, each with its own particular smell. In those days nothing was sold ready packaged - everything was selected by the customer and then wrapped. Thus there was always a hint of fish outside the fishmonger's shop, meat outside the butcher's, bread outside the baker's and so on. In the summertime there was more than a hint from some shops! Rippons the newsagents, on the corner of Threadneedle Street always had that strange but familiar smell of newsprint.

Our own shop smelled of coffee and bacon, mixed with the warm spiciness of nutmegs and cloves. On the other side of the Duke Street was one of my favourite aromas - that of the gloriously rich smell of leather which wafted into the street from the harness maker's shop. All the pubs gave forth the smell of beer, especially on market days when they were so crowded that the doors were always kept wide open.

Passing through Tindal Square and reaching the upper part of the High Street, my nose was assailed by what I can only describe as an unbelievably horrible stench! This emanated from the mysterious tallow factory, owned by Mr Budd, at the back of the shops on the east side of the High Street. Walking on quickly I soon came to something far more to my liking - the delicious aroma from the large shop and restaurant of Mr Hicks, the pastrycook and baker. There were, at that time, several wine shops in the High Street and my Wesleyan teetotal nose learned to distinguish between beer and wine at a very tender age. It was to be many, many years before my palate had the opportunity to develop the same skill!

Cramphorns, the corn merchants, had a pleasantly earthy smell which reminded me of my Grandfather Reynolds at Springfield. Even from the High Street, if the wind was in the right direction and the weather was warm, I would be aware of the slow-moving river with its own peculiar effluvium. On reaching the Stone Bridge, however, the smell of the river was masked by yet another smell. This was the unforgettable stench of Dixon's leather tannery, situated between the bridge and Baddow Road.

In Moulsham Street, there was such a conglomeration of smells in such a tightly packed area that it was hard to distinguish one from the other. Butchers', bakers', wet fish and fried fish shops mingled together. There was the unspeakable horror of Mr Palmer's slaughterhouse, a sinister lodging house and beer houses galore. Each had its own individual smell - some pleasant, many noisome and all memorable. Further up Moulsham Street was Godfrey's rope yard which gave forth a refreshingly pleasant aroma after the mixture of food, drink and animal smells. Godfrey's rope yard was almost at the southern limit of the town; beyond it there was little but the Chelmsford Union Workhouse. This may well have provided something for my nose to recognize, but it was too long a walk for my small legs!

It is hard to imagine now that each business could be identified by its own particular smell, pleasing or otherwise. Sounds, too, have changed. Chelmsford - in common with every town and village in the country - is far noisier now than in the far off days of my childhood; the internal combustion engine has seen to that. Yet the town was certainly not a quiet place; there was far too much going on for it to be so. Today's sounds are more homogenized and are dominated by the incessant sound of traffic.

There were, I feel, many more distinctive sounds when I was a boy. The horses' hooves made a particular sound as they trotted on the wooden block surfaces of streets in the town, but they made an almost deafening clatter on the stone setts of New Street. The hooves of the cattle could also be heard there as they were driven from the railway goods yard to the market, but they were usually drowned by the mooing of the poor, terrified beasts.

The various street traders each had their own distinctive sound with which to attract customers. Many of them shouted their wares, but for me the sweetest sound by far was the tinkling of the muffin man's bell.

I believe we were more aware of sounds in those days before the advent of even a cat's whisker wireless receiver. It was rare to hear music other than during Sunday services in church and chapel, or our own 'home-made' music.

Thus when the Italian hurdy-gurdy man stopped outside the Golden Fleece to entertain us, and the German boys' band or Salvation Army band set up a pitch in Tindal Square, we were delighted with all that they were able to give us.

Moulsham Street

THE TOWN FIRE BRIGADE

Of all the many and varied experiences of my childhood years, there is one which perhaps brings back more vivid memories than any other. It was the sound of the fire horn. The thrill of the strident blast of sound never palled, however often it occurred.

There were few people who lived as close to the Chelmsford Borough Fire Station as I did and I felt a great affection for the firemen and their horses.

Before the horn had sounded its last peremptory wail, onlookers began to stream towards the Fire Station by way of Duke Street, Threadneedle Street and Market Road. Superintendent Diaper lived in the Station House and was always in charge of the proceedings. The Station Officer was Mr Murkin; I remember him well as he always had a smile and a kind word for me. The crews of the two fire engines were all Council employees and lived in the neighbourhood. At the sound of the fire horn they dropped their work, wherever they were, and hurried on bicycles or on foot to the Fire Station. Here they would speedily change into their dark blue, thick serge tunics and trousers, their leather belts with axes and other tools, and finally put on their brightly shining helmets. One or both 'steamers' were drawn out onto the forecourt, the fireman in charge of the boiler having already lit the fire, which was always laid in advance with combustible material.

We stood as though mesmerized, watching the thick black smoke belching forth from the curiously shaped brass funnel and knowing that in a short time there would be sufficient pressure to activate the pump. In its turn the pump would give life to the water in the town's water pipes, ponds and rivers and transform it into a stream of water powerful enough to knock over anyone caught in its jet.

Waiting for the horses to be brought to the Fire Station was always an anxious time. The horses were kept in the Bell Meadow, next to the Corn Exchange, and on hearing the alarm the ostlers from the Bell Hotel hurried to the meadow to catch them and bring them to the Fire Station. Usually, though not always, the horses were co-operative and a cheer went up as they were led up Threadneedle Street. In a very short space of time the horses were 'put to' and the eight firemen were aboard, sitting four a side, back to back. Then, with the firemen still adjusting their uniforms and checking their equipment, the cavalcade of the Merryweather Steamer with separate fire escape and trucks laden with hoses moved off.

There was shouting and encouragement from the onlookers and the ringing of the firebell was surely loud enough to alert everyone in Chelmsford. As with the circus procession, the cavalcade was not complete without a crowd of men and boys following it. A fire, although potentially disastrous for those personally concerned, was a source of great interest (and probably entertainment!) to others and it seemed as though all those who could possibly do so followed the engine to enjoy the spectacle.

Superintendent Diaper would have worn a uniform similar to this

A TRAGIC SATURDAY AFTERNOON

Before the First World War members of the Essex Yeomanry paraded on Saturday afternoons for drill and riding practice. For this purpose horses were hired from various livery stables attached to sundry hotels and inns. Among these hotels was the Plough Hotel in Duke Street, just by the railway station. As was usual on these occasions, groups of boys hung about the stable yards, waiting for the return of the soldiers from their exercises and hoping to get a brief ride on one of the horses.

On this particular Saturday the usual routine was being carried out. Several lads were up in the saddles and thoroughly enjoying this brief excitement while the soldiers stood about stretching their legs and chatting to one another. For some unknown reason one of the horses decided to go into Railway Street. In a flash the horse was out of the yard with the lad breathing panic and tugging on the bit, but before the horse could be stopped it had slipped through the railway arch and into the forecourt of the station.

By this time the lad was thoroughly frightened and imparted his panic to the horse which quickly picked up speed and began to career down Duke Street towards Tindal Square.

I was in our shop with my father at the time. We caught a fleeting glimpse of the boy crouched low and clinging desperately onto the neck of the furiously galloping horse. Only a very few moments were needed for the terrified horse to continue through Tindal Square and straight across the High Street where it hurled itself through the photographic window of Fred Spalding's shop. The noise of the breaking glass was heard as far away as our shop!

For the following moment or two there was silence, but then life recommenced with shouts and the blowing of police whistles. One person (I believe her name was Miss Beckett) who had been looking in Fred Spalding's window was killed, while several others were injured by the flying glass.

And the horse and the boy? It was the horse which actually hit the window and went through, cutting itself to such an extent that it had to be put down, while the boy - still clinging to the horse's neck - went through the hole made by the horse and miraculously escaped with his life.

I shall never forget the expression on the boy's face as he and the horse passed our shop. I do not think I have ever experienced such a look of sheer, unmitigated terror since that day.

Postal Address:
4, HIGH STREET.

47

THE CORONATION OF GEORGE V AND QUEEN MARY

Of course the sun shone for this royal occasion on Wednesday, 22nd June, 1911! All my memories of the long day are of sunshine, heat and the scent of the short mown grass onto which we gladly flung ourselves from time to time. We had been told at school that committee meetings had been held to arrange the multiplicity of activities connected with the day's programme of events, together with such mundane necessities as extra lavatory accommodation and the care of lost children. No-one could possibly plead ignorance of the forthcoming excitements of Coronation Day. The Borough Council had risen to the occasion and had produced a definitive *Programme of Festivities* - an admirable piece of work full of details of all the events.

When I came downstairs to breakfast on the morning of that memorable day Mother gave me my *Programme of Festivities*. This had Father's name on it but my parents had decided that I should have it. I have cherished it ever since and have read every page many, many times. It included everything anyone could need or want to know about Coronation Day and even had one hundred and nineteen photographs of the town worthies from the Mayor downwards. What a collection - and all for tuppence!

After breakfast I went down the steep stairs into the shop just as Father was unlocking the heavy front doors. He left the blinds drawn as it was a Bank Holiday but the sunlight streamed through the south-facing doorway. I stepped out onto the pavement and saw, coming towards me, an extraordinary figure. A tall, thin man dressed from head to foot in scarlet and quite unlike anything I had ever seen before in my life. It was indeed a sinister figure, made even more so by a long, curling tail which ended in a bone arrowhead that clattered on the pavement. My father laughed at my amazement and told me that this devilish creature was none other than Mr Hall, the sign writer. Mr Hall was no stranger to me as he had recently re-painted Father's name above the shop but, even so, I could scarcely believe it was he.

Mr Hall stopped to chat with Father and explained that he was trying out his costume prior to the Grand Fancy Dress Parade and Competition which was to take place later in the day. He was, he said, actually finding his costume extremely uncomfortable and hot, even at eight o'clock in the morning! He sat on the step for a rest, then set off up Duke Street with his evil tail tapping on the pavement behind him.

In those far away days much more emphasis was placed on the religious nature of any occasion such as this. So it was that the morning was largely devoted to services of praise and prayer which were held in every church of every denomination. I went with my parents as usual to the Wesleyan Church but I think that on this occasion I was too excited and fidgety to take much notice of the service. All I wanted was to march in the Grand Procession! This was to be made up of a huge number of people, representing different aspects of the life of the town.

From eleven o'clock onwards the various processions made their way from all parts of Chelmsford, entering the Recreation Ground by way of London Road, Threadneedle Street, Park Road and New Writtle Street. The parades from the churches and chapels were augmented by military bands and by representatives of many secular organisations. As we came out of the church we marched towards the Rec where everyone was converging on the large meadow between the railway viaduct and Park Road.

As noon approached the final procession, that of His Worship the Mayor and sundry local dignitaries, arrived and took up its appointed place. The crowd fell silent and the clock of St Mary's church struck twelve. An impressive service was held and this time I must have concentrated to such an extent that I can still remember it with the utmost clarity. The service was presided over by the Right Reverend the Lord Bishop of Barking - how splendid he appeared with his robes and his mitre, especially when compared with our more soberly dressed Wesleyan ministers. I shall never forget the sound of those thousands of Chelmsfordians joining in with the hymns, "O God, our help in ages past" and "Now thank we all our God". The singing was accompanied by the combined bands of the Mid-Essex Regiment and the Salvation Army, and a truly wonderful volume of sound was produced.

No doubt countless similar services were being held up and down the country but for Chelmsford, with its recently-born wireless industry in its very midst, a dramatic conclusion had been planned. Immediately after the end of the service a detachment of the Essex RHA fired a twenty one gun salute and St Mary's bells pealed out joyfully. Then all eyes turned to the great metal Marconi mast, more than two hundred feet high, in Hall Street. A mighty cheer went up from the crowd as, from the top of one of the masts, a very large Union Jack slowly unfurled and then billowed out to its fullest extent. The significance of this was that the whole action had been set in motion by the Mayor who, on pressing a switch, had activated the unfurling of the Union Jack by remote wireless control. This wonderfully modern spectacle was surely peculiar to Chelmsford! As the flag fluttered against the blue sky the crowd, accompanied by the bands, sang the National Anthem with tremendous fervour.

From then onwards the day was one of jollification and light-hearted fun. I can see now from my programme that there were many events for people of all ages but, naturally, my memories are of those which concerned me personally. There was, for instance, dinner for the Old Folk in the Drill Hall but it is the

B H H. Mother. Edith, Arthur, and Father, 1910

picnic in the Rec which I remember well. The large picnic area was soon filled with a happy, hungry crowd of noisy families enjoying their food. The warmth of friendliness and happiness equalled that of the summer sunshine.

There was so much to see and do that we scarcely knew where to begin once we had finished our picnic. My parents were quite happy for me to spend the rest of the day with my school friends and I was more than pleased with this arrangement. Father would, he said, be in the Rec for much of the afternoon and evening but would slip back home from time to time. Mother would be at home for most of the time as by now I had a young brother and a baby sister who would probably be happier at home.

Tea was served for the children of the town's Elementary Schools but, as pupils of King Edward VI Grammar School, my friends and I did not qualify for this treat. Each of the Elementary School children was given a commemorative mug as a memento of this historic occasion. The supplier of these enamelled mugs to the Council was B H Harrison and Son, Ironmongers, and I suspect Uncle Walter allowed a few of the mugs to 'fall off the back of the cart' when being delivered. How very convenient! I was so pleased with my coronation mug that I have kept it all my life.

All sorts of entertainments and displays had been arranged for the afternoon, and among those which I recall enjoying the most were the Territorials' Display, the Decorated Bicycles and a Gymnastic Display by the boys of the Essex Home School.

By the time tea was over the evening's events were starting in earnest. My school friends and I could hardly believe that time was passing so quickly. Together we went from one attraction to another, determined to see and sample everything that was in the Rec. From time to time we would meet up with our parents for a moment, before being swept along in the crowd to the next display or entertainment. I had certainly never before been among such a vast crowd and, thinking back to that day, I remember the relaxed and good-humoured atmosphere.

The Fancy Dress Parade was a sight worth seeing; there were so many participants wearing the most outlandish variety of rig-outs. I looked in vain for Mr Hall in his red devil's costume as the parade wound its way through the Rec. I have often wondered if he managed to endure his discomfort for the whole day and, if so, whether he won a prize. How I wish that I had asked him when I next saw him but it is too late now.

Towards dusk a special display was given by the Chelmsford Fire Brigade. The men gave a fine demonstration of fire drill which involved the use of hoses and much water. The steamer was going fit to burst - so much steam had to be built up to draw the water from the lake. Then it was time for the climax of the display, a rescue from a house on fire, and for this purpose a dummy house had been built near the viaduct.

There was a great deal of smoke and noise but not much fire at first. We boys hoped to see the building really blazing! The fire escape was run up the side of the house and, to the accompaniment of cheers from the crowd, a body was brought safely down the long, whipping ladder. At last the house was seen to be fully alight and flames poured from the windows and the roof. This was the moment we had been waiting for! The whole Brigade went into action with every conceivable piece of fire-fighting equipment they could lay their hands on. In spite of their concerted efforts the house blazed away merrily - which was not surprising as most of it was wood!

The burning house was a great success but we could not linger too long as another spectacle, too good to be missed, was in store. We hurried towards the flagstaff, near which an enormous white screen had been erected. The proprietor of the Picture House in New Writtle Street had arranged to show moving pictures of the actual processions, crowds and scenes in the streets of London, together with views of Westminster Abbey. The films had been rushed down to Chelmsford from Liverpool Street by train and were duly shown in the gathering darkness. The applause was tumultuous!

Darkness fell but few people were yet making for home as almost everyone wanted to stay for the Grand Firework Display, due to begin at a quarter past ten. At this point my father spotted me so we stood together on a slight rise in what was then the top football field. From there we had an excellent view of the fireworks, which were let off down by the river. The hush of expectancy was suddenly shattered by the sound of a rapid cannonade far up in the sky. Then followed such a concentration of fireworks; I could never in my wildest dreams have imagined such a display! There were brightly coloured rockets, each one seeming to soar higher into the sky than the last, stately Roman candles, showers of golden rain and giant Catherine wheels spinning round on high structures. A dozen or more brilliant flares suspended on parachutes moved slowly over the town, lighting up every detail with their harsh white light.

The firework display drew to a close. For a moment there was darkness and comparative silence. Then, a few seconds later, there was a blaze of golden light on the scaffolding which had been specially built for the finale. Portraits of King George V and Queen Mary appeared in fireworks, surrounded by a golden frame of dazzling light and colour! As the brilliance faded we knew that this really was the end of the day. And what a day it had been!

Father and I walked across Park Road, along the cinder path past the Museum into Market Road, along King Edward Avenue and into Threadneedle Street. As we were nearing Market Road I was aware of music coming from the

Drill Hall and asked Father what was happening. He told me that the Grand Coronation Ball was just being opened by the Mayor and Mayoress and would last until three o'clock in the morning. I begged to be allowed to watch the proceedings for a short while, but Father was adamant. "Certainly not", he replied. "It's not for the likes of us - the tickets cost eighteen pence each and refreshments are extra. What's more, some of us have to work tomorrow!"

Later, having had some supper and gone at last to bed, I lay thinking of all the lovely things I could buy for eighteen pence - sherbet suckers, liquorice bootlaces, pear-shaped gob-stoppers, aniseed balls and ... and ... I must have fallen asleep, for the next thing I knew was that the church clock was striking seven and that the sunlight was streaming across the churchyard. It was a new day and the beginning of the reign of King George and Queen Mary.

Borough of   Chelmsford.

ALDERMAN T. J. D. CRAMPHORN, Mayor.

CORONATION OF

KING GEORGE V. & QUEEN MARY

Official Programme

OF

CELEBRATION IN CHELMSFORD

ON

THURSDAY, JUNE 22nd, 1911.

J. O. THOMPSON, Hon. Sec.

Printed and Published at the "Essex County Chronicle" Office,
98 High Street, Chelmsford.

Title page of Coronation programme. 1911

MISS BIRD'S SCHOOL

It had been in 1906, five years before the King's Coronation, that I became a timid schoolboy and began my ten years of formal education. Miss Bird's School was at 25, New London Road, opposite the Congregational Church. It was the most westerly house in the terrace of tall, substantial Victorian dwellings - the most easterly being the Chelmsford Institute.

Miss Anna Bird, a strict and evangelical spinster, was always dressed in black with perhaps just a dash of colour on her mantle. She never appeared without a small starched head-dress. There were two assistant teachers in the school, namely Mrs King and Miss Smee. Miss Smee was much the youngest of the three and was loved by all the pupils. We loved her so much in our youthful way especially when she wept, which she did frequently. Miss Bird was, I believe, particularly severe in her handling of this young and pretty pupil teacher. Our sympathies naturally always lay with the lovely Miss Smee and our boyish hearts bled when she was distressed.

I suppose there must have been about three dozen pupils in the school and I think we used the entire building. I have no idea where Miss Bird lived, but I always imagined that she spent her whole time in the schoolrooms and had no need of the food or sleep upon which ordinary mortals were dependent!

On my first day at school I was escorted by Mother through Tindal Square, along Tindal Street and into New London Road. There, having checked that I was still clean and tidy, Mother led me up the two or three steps to the front door and handed me over to Miss Bird. After that first morning I was considered sufficiently sensible to make my way to school without adult company. The other pupils, too, always walked to and from school unaccompanied by parents.

One of the joys of the walk to school was passing the antique shop owned by Mr John Gosling. This delightful establishment was in the middle of the same terrace as the school and I would hurry along so that I had plenty of time to gaze rapturously at the window display before entering the school. The shop window was constantly filled with all sorts of fascinating articles, one of which I coveted with a great longing. This was a framed painting of a riverside scene and a man fishing. There must have been more to the picture than met the eye for with monotonous regularity the fisherman jerked his rod and brought a fish from the water! Every afternoon, on my way home from school, I would watch the fisherman again and wish that the picture were mine.

It was still in the window when I left Miss Bird's School and some ten years later, when I was seventeen, Mr Gosling's premises came under the auctioneer's hammer. I obtained a sale catalogue and read it from cover to cover. In vain I searched among the list of three hundred and fifty items for the picture but,

<u>Removed for Convenience of Sale.</u>

The Mart, Chelmsford.

A Catalogue of the

STOCK-IN-TRADE

Of an Antique and Curio Dealer, by instructions of Mr. John Gosling, who is
leaving Chelmsford ; also a quantity of Capital

HOUSEHOLD FURNITURE

And Effects, including Kitchen Table and Chairs, China and Glass, Pictures,
Linoleum and Rugs, Lady's and Gent.'s Easy Chairs, Couches, Dining Chairs,
Mahogany Dining Table, Overmantels,

TWO PIANOFORTES,

Roll-top Desk, Dining Room Suite, Two Oak Adjustable Chairs, Bedsteads,
Mattresses, Wardrobes, Dressing Tables and Washstands, Dressing Glasses,
Feather Beds, Toilet Sets, Two Mowers, and numerous other Effects.

FRED. TAYLOR & CO.

(GILBERT WILKS & ALBERT F. WHITE)

Will Sell the above by Auction, at **The Mart, 17, Duke Street,
Chelmsford**, on

Thursday, Sept. 27th, 1917,

At 11 a.m. precisely.

Auction Offices: 17, Duke Street, Chelmsford.

Printed by the "Essex Weekly News" Series, Limited, Chelmsford.

Sale of John Gosling's effects

55

sadly, it was not there. Perhaps Mr Gosling could not bear to part with it and had taken it to his new home. I shall never know, but I do believe I would have spent all the money I had in the world on it.

Entry to the school was always through the front door and the hall. There was also a steep, short flight of steps from the pavement down to a glass door in the area, but this was never used by the pupils. The basement rooms had probably been used originally as a breakfast room and kitchen. The latter was still used as such when I was a pupil and dinner was prepared there by the domestic servant - a harassed, thin woman who always looked as though she could benefit from a good meal herself. She served dinner in the breakfast room for the three teachers and those boys and girls who, for various reasons, had to eat their dinner under the stern, watchful eye of Miss Bird. Most of the children, myself included, lived close enough to go home at dinner time.

The breakfast room was used as a classroom in the mornings and afternoons, but was quickly transformed into a dining room at mid-day. By the time I returned for the afternoon session, all evidence of the meal had been speedily removed into the kitchen by the domestic servant.

The breakfast room and kitchen were on the same level as the rectangular garden which was mainly carpeted with gravel and furnished with trestle tables and wooden forms. This was used as an out-of-doors classroom in fine, warm weather. Upstairs, on the ground floor, the two former reception rooms were used as form rooms. These two rooms were referred to by Miss Bird as the dining room and the drawing room.

The dining room looked out on to New London Road, while the drawing room had a good view of the garden. As was so often the case in this type of Victorian house, these two rooms were separated by folding wooden doors or screens which when opened and folded back made one sizeable room.

The screens were always opened up for the morning service with which every day began. Having wished her staff and pupils 'Good morning', Miss Bird seated herself at the harmonium and accompanied the first hymn. This was followed by a passage from the Bible, read by Mrs King or Miss Smee. The prayers, which seemed to last for ever, were always led by Miss Bird who then returned to the harmonium for the closing hymn. At the end of the service Miss Bird dismissed us, two of the older pupils closed the screens and it was time for school work to begin in real earnest.

The older girls thundered up the stairs into the former bedrooms and the younger girls settled down in the drawing room. The older boys had their lessons in the dining room, while we younger lads went downstairs to the breakfast room. It was always dark and gloomy there; perhaps that was why we worked at the trestle table in the garden when the weather was suitable.

The list of subjects taught was far from extensive. I still have my termly report for the summer of 1908 and reading it now I see how narrow the curriculum was, even for those days. There was a great emphasis on the 3Rs, reading, writing and arithmetic.

The report shows that the subjects I was learning at that time were Scripture, Grammar, Geography, Orthography (spelling), Arithmetic, Writing, Reading and Drill. The comment for each subject was written and initialled by Miss Bird, as by 1908 I was one of the older boys and therefore had the doubtful privilege of being in her class.

She also reported that my neatness was 'very satisfactory' and my general conduct 'good'. I doubt I would have ever dared to let it be otherwise! Even for relatively young children, detention was an acceptable form of punishment. I am happy to say that Miss Bird wrote a firm '0' in the spaces for Lateness, Detentions and Returned Lessons on my report.

I still have all my handwriting exercise books, in the earliest of which I practised drawing pot hooks and learned how to make a straight line. Then I progressed to individual letters and then to three letter words. Each page was divided into eight lines; the first and fifth lines had letters or words printed on them and the remaining lines were to be completed by the pupil. Each book has been dated at the end, presumably by the teacher, but is totally devoid of any words of praise for all my hours of hard work. In fact the only comments are critical ones such as 'Basil was careless' and 'Not good'. Looking at my school reports from Miss Bird it seems I was a fairly industrious and intelligent pupil and I wonder why such a very negative approach was adopted.

Two of my handwriting books, dated 1908, contained phrases to copy. The phrases in one book are mainly definitions of geographical terms, including such useful facts as 'Zephyr, a soft mild wind' and 'Glaciers are rivers of ice'. The other book ensured that I would always remember such tongue twisters as 'Sago is the inner pith of a palm' and 'Groats are oats set free from husks'. Having copied them in my book at least six times I have never forgotten them!

I have no recollection of being actually taught to read and can only assume that as Miss Bird accepted no pupils under the age of six years, most children could already read by the time they started school. As for our arithmetic lessons, we spent the whole time either chanting multiplication tables or laboriously doing addition, subtraction, multiplication and division sums on our slates. I doubt whether I had any idea of the meaning of these processes, but at least the tables and number bonds were firmly in my head and have stayed there for more than eighty years!

The use of the garden for lessons makes me think that Miss Bird was aware of the merits of fresh air. Miss Smee took drill classes which were held in the garden whenever possible. We stood in lines, trying our hardest to follow the exercises which Miss Smee demonstrated at the front of the class. Her Edwardian clothes and her modesty must have restricted her range of movements and consequently those of her pupils who copied her so faithfully. Despite this we all loved the drill lessons and I can still remember some of the exercises and the chant that went with one of them,

> 'Drill, drill, drill,
> One, two, three,
> Makes my back so
> Straight you see.'

Yet, in spite of all the primitive teaching methods then in vogue the majority of us satisfied Miss Bird and our parents by gaining for entry to one of the two main schools in the town, namely, King Edward VI Grammar School or the newly-opened High School for Girls.

SCHOOL FOR GIRLS,

Age quod agis

25, LONDON ROAD, CHELMSFORD.

REPORT for the *Summer* Term, 1908

Name *Basil Harrison* Class Containing Girls, average age

SUBJECTS.	RANK.	Remarks on Work.	SIGNATURE OF TEACHER.
SCRIPTURE		*Attentive shows intelligence*	*AB*
GRAMMAR		*A careful little pupil*	*AB*
COMPOSITION			
LITERATURE			
GEOGRAPHY		*Has a fair knowledge of Geographical*	*AB*
ORTHOGRAPHY		*Satisfactory* *Definition*	*AB*
ELEMENTARY SCIENCE			
ARITHMETIC		*Dealing satisfactory progress shows ability*	*AB*
ALGEBRA			
WRITING		*Writes with care*	*AB*
DRAWING	*reading*	*Reads distinctly & with expression*	*AB*
PAINTING			
FRENCH			
SINGING			
DRILL		*Good*	*AB*
CHIP CARVING			
NEEDLEWORK			
GENERAL CONDUCT		*Good*	*AB*
NEATNESS		*Very satisfactory*	*AB*

Number of Times Absent   Number of Times detained 0

   ,,   ,,   Late 0   ,,   Lessons returned

School report, 1908

PRINCIPAL *Anna Bird*

NEXT TERM BEGINS *Sep 15* 1908

58

CARTE DE VISITE PORTRAIT

B H H in King Edward School uniform, photographed in St Mary's churchyard, 1908

KING EDWARD VI GRAMMAR SCHOOL

The great day had come at last! From now on I was to be a fully fledged schoolboy, having left Miss Bird's School behind me. So it was that on a Monday morning in September, 1908, I accompanied my fifteen year old cousin, Cyril, along Duke Street and Broomfield Road. Cyril had assured my anxious mother that he would show me where the new boys were to go and, no doubt, he could hardly wait to be rid of me.

I still remember the uncomfortable, sinking feeling in the region of my stomach as we passed the front of the school and entered the sacred confines by the large, heavy north gate. We walked together up the side of the classrooms and there Cyril left me in the midst of a crowd of new boys looking just as apprehensive as I felt. Soon we were ushered into a classroom and told to wait quietly. There was no need to stress the word 'quietly'; we were all too scared to raise our voices.

Suddenly the door flew open and in strode a seemingly tremendous figure of a man, with a black gown swirling around him and a black mortar board in the crook of his arm. (Why on earth, I wondered as we all trembled in our seats, had I ever considered Miss Bird frightening?)

I soon learned that this awe-inspiring man was none other than the Headmaster - Mr Frank W Rogers, BA (Trinity College, Dublin). He stood on the low platform and proceeded to look us over. All at once he galvanised us by uttering in a loud voice "Good morning, boys", to which we responded with an extremely feeble salutation.

This was not improved upon by the sound of several voices saying from habit "Good morning, Miss"! Mr Rogers appeared to be roused into a fury, though no doubt this happened with every group of new boys. He insisted that the whole performance must be gone through again - and correctly this time. So out he went, slamming the door behind him and returning a moment later to greet us once more. This time our response was more confident and the great man was satisfied at last.

In the meantime several other masters dressed in academic gowns and carrying mortar boards had strolled into the room to allocate the new boys to the four houses - Holland, Mildmay, Tindal and Strutt. The masters looked us over as I had seen the farmers in the cattle market inspect pens of pigs. Thank goodness we were not subjected to prods from sticks as the poor pigs were! To my complete surprise I found myself chosen fairly early on by the House Master of Holland. I cannot believe that I had much in my favour and I certainly did not look as though I would be a potential asset on the football field. I can only think that I did not threaten to be too much of a troublemaker. So it was that

KING EDWARD'S SCHOOL, CHELMSFORD.

TERMINAL REPORT _Spring_ TERM, 1909

Name _Harrison B.H._   Form _I_

Number of Boys in Form _15_   Order in Form _8_

SUBJECT.	ORDER.	MASTER'S REMARKS.	MASTER'S INITIALS.
Divinity		He shews an intelligent interest in the lessons on our Lord's life.	I.B.
Reading and Poetry	4	I am pleased with his work, he reads & recites very nicely.	M.K.
Composition and Writing	8	His attempt at improvement in writing have been successful. Composition fair.	M.B.
Grammar	5	His progress is quite satisfactory. He answers thoughtfully & with care.	M.Y.S.
Spelling	4	Very good, he gets very few faults in dictation.	M.B.
History	8	Has laid the foundation for a very good knowledge of History	H.M.
Geography	9	& Geography. Work well and answers very intelligently	H.M.
French			
Arithmetic	10	Rather slow in learning new rules & inaccurate in his workings.	M.B.
Musical Drill		He drills very well & keeps good time.	M.B.
Art	4	He is becoming more skilful in the use of pencil & brush.	M.B.

Number of times absent,	0	Number of times "On Report,"	0
Number of times late,	0	Half Holidays lost	0 out of _11_
Number of times detained,	2	Merit Holidays gained,	2 out of 2

General Conduct _Good_

The School re-assembles at _9_ a.m. on ~~Thurs~~ _Wed_ day _May 2th 5th_ 190 ~~6~~9 when all Boys are expected to return. Absence at the beginning of a Term, excepting in case of sickness, must be made good.

Goodbye.
Grow up as you are now a

M. Benson Form Mistress.

J. W. Roelse M.A., Head Master

School report. 1909

I proudly wore my school cap with its large blue star of Holland and the metal school badge stitched onto the front. In summer the ribbon around my straw boater showed that I belonged to Holland House. I still have my school badge among my treasured possessions.

Once the selection had been completed and every boy assigned to a House, we were eventually herded up the main stone stairway and into the school hall. What a vast hall this was to my eyes - it seemed as large as the nave of St Mary's Church. We were assembled at the west end of the hall, where the necessary number of forms with sloping desks attached had already been prepared for us. This section of the school hall was to be our form room and we were introduced to our form master. Our master (and I could hardly believe this) was Miss Benson! What a contrast to the stern, gruff masters we had already encountered. Miss Benson was gentle and kind and, before the day was over, every boy in the form adored her.

I made a big mistake in the school yard on my first day and I still blush with embarrassment when I remember my naïvety. My cousin Hubert was a few months older than I and had already been at the Grammar School for a term or so. Catching sight of him in the school yard, I ran towards him and called "Hubert, Hubert, hallo!" He turned to me with a look of horror, his fist shot out and landed on my nose and the next thing I knew I was on the ground with my collar and tie torn off! I had learned an important lesson that day. Never address anyone in school by their Christian name!

Mr Rogers, although he gave us new boys such a harsh introduction to grammar school life, had much on the credit side. He had been appointed Head Master in 1885 when the school was in a poor way and this must have been just the incentive he needed. My father was a pupil when Mr Rogers took over the school at the old site in Duke Street. Father used to speak of the changes that took place, of Mr Roger's tremendous energy and his enthusiasm for providing a broad education for all the boys in his care.

The number and variety of new activities attracted many of the pupils - theatrical performances, magic lantern lectures, sports fixtures and concerts were among the regular happenings. The versatile Headmaster composed much of the music for these concerts; he sang in his fine baritone voice and also conducted the school orchestra. Nothing, it seemed, happened in the school that was not motivated by Mr Rogers. There were societies galore - Debating, Athletics, Swimming, Choral, Orchestral, Cycling and many others.

Perhaps the greatest memorial of all to Mr Rogers was the erection of the new Grammar School in Broomfield Road in 1892 and the consequent abandonment of the dilapidated Duke Street premises. The new premises had accommodation for twenty-four boarders and one hundred and twenty-six day

King Edward VI. Grammar School,

CHELMSFORD.

Speech Day, July 28, 1910.

DONORS OF PRIZES.

MR. H. I. CHAPMAN.
MR. C. CROMPTON.
MR. P. J. DEBNAM.
MR. W. DENNIS.
MR. W. W. DUFFIELD.
MRS. HARRISON GRAY.
MR. W. H. HARRISON.
MR. A. G. HODGSON.
REV. CANON H. E. HULTON.
REV. CANON H. A. LAKE.

MR. H. F. PASH.
REV. F. S. PAYNTER
  (Fritz Paynter Memorial Prize for Scripture).
MISS E. RIDLEY.
MR. C. E. RIDLEY.
MR. W. STUNT.
REV. CANON O. W. TANCOCK.
MR. J. O. THOMPSON.
MRS. USBORNE.
LIEUT.-COLONEL G. W. WOOD.

PATRONS of the LITERARY and ATHLETIC CLUBS.

HIS WORSHIP THE MAYOR (ALDERMAN CRAMPHORN).

MR. F. CHANCELLOR.
MRS. DOBSON.
MR. W. W. DUFFIELD.
MR. R. FRANKLIN.
MRS. GREENALL.
REV. CANON H. E. HULTON.
MRS. JACKSON.
REV. CANON H. A. LAKE.

MR. J. B. PASH.
MR. OWEN PARRY.
REV. F. S. PAYNTER.
MR. FRED TAYLOR.
MR. W. G. WENLEY.
MRS. WILDE.
LIEUT.-COLONEL G. W. WOOD.
THE HEADMASTER.

PRINTED AT THE "ESSEX COUNTY CHRONICLE" OFFICE, CHELMSFORD.

Speech day. 1910

boys. This soon proved to be insufficient space for the growing number of pupils and plans for enlarging the building were drawn up and put into action.

I must now move on from my father's time at the Grammar School to my own time there, as an eight year old in the Preparatory Department. I shall never forget the way Mr Rogers used to burst into the hall where we were sitting quietly at our desks listening to Miss Benson. With his arms stretched out like great black wings under his gown, and accompanied by Yum-Yum his small, silky Pomeranian with its black tongue hanging out, Mr Rogers would throw the waste paper basket the length of the hall for the dog to retrieve. How we loved these antics! Sometimes he would bring some little novelty to show us and would hold it up and sing,   "Here is a thing, a very pretty thing.

What shall we do with this funny little thing?"

Then, just as suddenly as he had arrived, he would disappear through the door with Yum-Yum. After this brief interruption Miss Benson would always say quietly, "Now, boys, let's get on with the lesson'.

The daily service known as School Prayers was held every morning and, as at Miss Bird's School, there was a set pattern for this. The wooden forms, each holding eight boys, stretched the entire length of the hall from east to west. Facing the boys, against the south wall, was the huge dais from which the Headmaster would conduct Prayers.

The service was never dull, perhaps because Mr Rogers conducted the whole of it himself in his usual flamboyant fashion. I never recall any participation from the teachers. He also accompanied the hymns on the organ and would play several florid chords before the introduction to the first hymn. This was to ensure that the two boys chosen to pump the bellows were wide awake and ready to provide enough wind for the organ to produce its maximum volume. At the end of the service a loud and exuberant outgoing voluntary was played while we filed back to our places for the day's lessons to begin.

On one particular morning the routine was unfolding in the usual way with the forms being gradually filled up by the boys. As the clock crept towards nine the masters and Miss Benson filed in from their common room. At nine o'clock precisely Mr Rogers appeared in the doorway and taking off his mortar board with a wide sweep of his arm placed it on the unsuspecting head of a small boy! The boy (I have long since forgotten his name) stood crimson-faced with embarrassment while Mr Rogers proceeded to walk a complete lap of the hall. As he approached the innocent lad he raised his right arm and, with a flick of his wrist, took the mortar board and sent it spinning in a huge parabola across the hall. One brave boy picked it up, dusted it and handed it back to the Headmaster who, to the amazement of us all, was laughing! Never had there been such 'goings-on' at Miss Bird's!

King Edward VI.'s School,

CHELMSFORD.

The *Summer* Term will commence on *May 11th 1916*

Parents are particularly requested either to send a cheque or cash in payment of Tuition fees to the Clerk to the Governors at or before the commencement of the Term.

All boys are required to be in attendance at 9 o'clock on the morning of the opening day.

Boys whose parents so desire can dine in the Head - Master's house, the charge being £2 per Term.

The Tuition fees are as follows :—

For boys under 12	...	...	£2 15s. 10d. per Term.
For boys over 12	...	...	£3 15s. 10d. „ „

These fees cover all subjects of instruction included in the curriculum and the use of all educational apparatus necessary for those subjects except such printed books and mathematical instruments as may be required by parents or guardians to become their property.

The Head-Master particularly requests that all boys shall (1) be provided with the School Cap and Badge for wearing in the Playground, and on coming to and returning from School ; and (2) bring back the Health Paper carefully filled in, on returning to School.

Every boy on returning to School after absence during the Term is required to bring with him a letter from his parent or guardian explaining the reason for such absence.

The Head-Master will be pleased to see Parents and others on Wednesday in each week during the Term between the hours of twelve and one, or on Saturdays between the hours of nine and ten. It is requested that they will not call upon him on other days during School hours without making an appointment.

Notice ˙in writing must be given to the Clerk to the Governors within one calendar month after the commencement of the Term at the end of which it is proposed to withdraw any boy from the School, or the Tuition fees for the ensuing Term must be paid. In the case of Boarders a full Term's notice in writing must be given to the Head-Master previous to the withdrawal of any boy from the House or the Boarding fees for the ensuing Term must be paid.

Cheques for Fees, except Boarding fees, must be made payable to

WILLIAM STUNT,

Clerk to the Governors.

71, Duke Street,
       Chelmsford.

Scale of fees, 1916

King Edward School, Form 2, Mr Dixon. 1909

B H H middle row on left with Holland star on cap. Admiral's Park, 1909

I had only been at the school for a year when Mr Rogers tendered his resignation, packed his bags and moved away from Chelmsford. He had achieved a great deal in his twenty-four years as Headmaster and I feel that my father and I were privileged to have both attended the school during this period.

Returning to school in September, 1909, there were changes to which both staff and pupils had to adapt. Our new Headmaster was Mr Thomas Hay, MA (Cantab) BSc (London), no newcomer to the Grammar School, having been senior science master from 1899 to 1903. He became an immediate success, helped in many ways by Mrs Hay, who was always ready with her violin to assist in any musical activity. Gone were the days of excitement and exuberance - Mr Hay exuded an atmosphere of calm and serenity.

I was now in Form 1 under Mr Dixon and following a much wider curriculum. I soon found that I was sorely lacking in Mental Arithmetic. Chanting tables by rote at Miss Bird's had not equipped me for solving simple mathematical problems - I had absolutely no idea how to apply the four rules. In English and in Reading, however, I could hold my own. In my eight years at the Grammar School I won just one award, for English when I was ten years old. The prize was a beautifully bound and tooled leather-covered volume with the school badge embossed in silver on the front. It was *The Life of Washington.* I wonder who chose it, and why? I have not yet read it and I doubt I ever shall.

So I moved up the school, passing through the hands of Mr Powley, Mr Wintle, Mr Galleymore, Mr Jervis and Mr Squire. Each of these masters had a different approach and no doubt each was competent but the two to whom I responded best were Mr Powley and Mr Dixon.

An incident from my days in Mr Powley's form has stuck in my mind throughout the years. One day a boy asked Mr Powley what was the large leather-bound book he was studying and Mr Powley replied that it was an old admission register dating back to the 1880s. The boy with curiosity then wanted to know whose was the first name in the register. Mr Powley turned to the first page and read aloud, "Harrison, Herbert John, 65 High Street", and looking at me enquired if it was a relative of mine. I proudly replied "Yes, Sir - my father", which Mr Powley then expressed to be a remarkable coincidence.

Mr Hay soon made his mark as Headmaster and this quiet, conscientious man was well-liked by the boys and, presumably, by the staff. He had none of his predecessor's dramatic, extrovert personality but he nevertheless made a great impact on the school. It was an exciting time for us all when electric light was installed throughout the premises as many of us did not have such a modern facility in our own homes.

Perhaps Mr Hay's greatest achievement during the years in which I was at the school was promoting a fund to raise sufficient money to acquire new playing

Essex Artillery in Chelmsford High Street, 1909

Tent No. 8, Annual Cadet camp, 1916

fields. On 13th June, 1914, Newfields, on the east side of Broomfield Road, was formally opened by Lord Kenyon of Boreham House.

To say that I was happy during this period of my life would be an understatement. The whole concept of school and learning was a thoroughly relaxed and pleasurable experience. None of us had any worry about finding work once we had left school, for the majority of our fathers were in business and would be glad to have their sons working with them. In my form alone there were sons of a butcher, a tailor, a shoemaker, a draper, a chemist, an inn keeper and, of course, a grocer. There were a few academically inclined boys but most seemed quite happy to just jog along and either take minor exams or none at all.

The Cadet Corps, which had been formed by Mr Rogers in 1904, was very popular. One afternoon each week was given over to cadet training, and I believe it was a good form of discipline as well as being physically challenging. The annual camp was an eye-opener to those boys who, like me, led a fairly sheltered and comfortable life at home for the rest of the year. A photograph of me with my fellow occupants of Tent 8, taken at the cadet camp in 1916, makes it appear that we were thoroughly enjoying this different lifestyle. In my diary for 28th October, 1915, I wrote "We had bayonet fighting in the Cadet Corps for the first time". Looking back, I see just how young and naïve we were as we carried out bayonet practice. I, at any rate, little thought that in a couple of years I might be doing this in the harsh reality of the battlefields of Flanders. Looking at the photograph of myself in my cadet uniform in 1915, I am amazed how tall I look! The photographer must have known exactly how to angle his camera to make each boy appear taller and older than he really was.

The last three years were particularly happy ones for me. Mr Hay had a natural gift for finding suitable tasks for the older boys and he asked me to overhaul the map library. This was a task I thoroughly enjoyed and Mr Hay seemed very satisfied with what I did. It led me to a deep interest in maps of all kinds and I spent many happy hours poring over them in the school library.

Another daily task allotted to me was that of school timekeeper. At the end of each period I would excuse myself from the classroom, go to the lobby to ring the electric bell and then nip across the quad to pull the long chain to operate the swinging bell in the little turret. From there I would hurry into the main school where, on the windowsill immediately opposite the Headmaster's study, the gong was kept. There was real skill in sounding it properly. The music had to be wooed from it very gently so that as the soft-headed drumstick touched the edge of the gong the notes blended and grew into a riot of sound. A final flourish on the very centre - and that was that. How I loved every minute of it!

Sadly the day came eventually, on 20th December, 1916, when I sounded the gong for the last time. My schooldays were over.

B H H in Cadet uniform, 1915

EARNING MY OWN LIVING

My father was adamant that on leaving school I should not immediately join him in the grocery business. He felt that it would be better for me to have some training as a clerk and, through his friendship with Mr Phillips of Strutt and Parker, I was invited to attend an interview with the Peel River Land & Mineral Company Ltd, which was based in New South Wales, but had registered offices in the City of London. There was no doubt in my mind that this was a terrific adventure! My excitement must have been infectious and I believe my parents were nearly as excited as I when I was offered a post with the company. I had grand ideas of going to live in London with its bright lights and its pavements of gold, but my parents soon put a stop to such fanciful thinking! Their opinion on this matter was, they assured me, due to the increased danger of air raids in the capital but I am sure there were other reasons too. In retrospect I have never regretted staying here in Chelmsford, where I belong. I started work in London on 30th December, 1916, at the age of sixteen and a half years.

The Peel River Company paid for my three monthly season ticket and I proudly collected this from the ticket office at the station: the cost was £1/13/1d - a great sum of money to me at the time. I was dressed in the obligatory city uniform of grey three piece suit, dark overcoat, gloves and bowler hat, it having been made perfectly clear by my employer that this was how I was to be attired every day. As it was only just after Christmas when I started work we still had relatives staying with us in Duke Street and, when I returned home after my first day, they were impressed by my bowler hat! It was the centre of attention and I had to don and doff it many times during the course of the evening!

As my first month at work drew to a close I looked forward with increasing anticipation to my first pay packet. On 31st January I received the princely sum of £3/9/- and felt a rich man as I emptied it out onto the kitchen table when I reached home. Now, I felt, the world was my oyster! Following Father's advice, however, I did some careful budgeting and, having paid Mother for my bed and board, still had enough money left for all I considered necessary as well as saving up for a new bicycle.

The town's cinemas - the Picture House and the Regent - were increasingly popular and the silent films they showed were a wonderful evening's entertainment. It was not uncommon to find a lengthy queue outside the cinema, but it was worth waiting to see such masterpieces as *Vendetta*, *Intolerance*, *My Old Dutch* and Charlie Chaplin in *Charlie by the Sea*. I occasionally went to the same film two or three times on consecutive nights for the sheer pleasure of it! I see from my diary for March, 1918, that I never managed to see *The Whip* as, by the time I arrived home from work each

9 Duke Street shortly before demolition

Photograph taken by B H H from west door of Cathedral in 1927.

White building on left is 9 Duke Street

evening that week, there was not a chance of getting into the Regent.

After five months at work I had saved enough money to buy the bicycle I had long been admiring in the window of Mr Cass's bicycle shop in the High Street. I had spent much time reading about the merits of the various makes of bicycles and had finally decided on a Raleigh. It was in the middle of May that I collected my gleaming bike from Mr Cass and cycled out to the south west of the town, through Writtle and Highwood to Blackmore. To my disappointment I felt a slight bumpiness and on inspection of the tyres found I had a slow puncture. With frequent stops and much use of the pump, however, I managed to reach home without the indignity of having to get off and push. My bike was perhaps my most important possession at that time as it enabled me to get out of the town and to explore the surrounding villages. I developed an interest in architecture and spent many happy Saturdays looking around the wide variety of parish churches in Essex. I also found that cycling was 'my' sport and, at the age of seventy-six I still enjoy being on my bicycle!

I had a pay rise after six months with the Peel River Company and the extra shilling in my pay packet made a significant difference. As the proud earner of £3/10/- per month I planned my Christmas shopping with care and on 15th December set off down Duke Street with my list. I was able to buy everything I wanted for relatives and friends in two of Chelmsford's well-known shops, Spalding's and Clarke's.

There could be no doubt, however, that the War dominated this period of every person's life. During the course of my work in London I experienced a number of heavy raids on the City and spent many hours in the basement with my colleagues. My diaries for the years 1915, 1917 and 1918 record news of the war - both national and local. Father, speaking to customers all day long, was in a prime position to hear any Chelmsford news and would always share it with me during the evening. Thus it was that I entered in my diary such incidents as the escape from the gaol of two German officers in May, 1917, and their sub-sequent recapture at Basildon. There were nights when we slept little due to air raids, and there was often sad news to come to terms with, such as the death of one of Alderman J O Thompson's sons, killed in action at the very end of 1917.

During the Great War there were many nights when our sleep was disturbed. One of those I remember especially clearly was the night of Friday, 28th September, 1917. The firing that I heard that night was the closest and heaviest I had so far experienced in Chelmsford. It seemed to be coming from the south but from how far away it was impossible to tell. The next day I heard that a Zeppelin had been shot down at Billericay, only nine miles away. That day was a Saturday and, although I longed to go to the scene of action, I had to go to work in London for the morning. At the first possible opportunity, on my arrival home from work, I cycled over to Billericay to see for myself the remains of the Zeppelin still lying where it had crashed. I picked up a small piece of fabric and a tiny fragment of metal as a reminder of that dreadful night.

I think it brought home to me the frailty of all those young men involved in the conflict in a way that nothing else had done. I had heard names of the dead read out at school, in church and spoken of by colleagues and friends, but until now the war had never seemed so real or so close. I was very conscious that it was less than ten months until my eighteenth birthday when I, too, would be eligible to fight and perhaps to die for my country.

There were inevitably changes in the town. It was in October, 1917, that I saw for the first time the Saracen's Head motor being driven by coal gas. Fuel shortages had begun to affect bus services earlier that year. Most operators had cut services but some had experimented with alternative fuels. The owner of the Saracen's Head was clearly anxious to maintain his service to and from the railway station. Early in 1918 I wrote in my diary that, while out for a walk with the family, we had passed the horsemeat shop. The meat had been cut and displayed with none of the care practised by my Uncle Tom on Springfield Hill, and we shuddered at the thought of having to eat it.

At the end of May, 1918, one of Father's old errand boys, Stanley Wood, was killed at the front. Father and Mother had been fond of Stanley and were naturally upset at his death. Although they said little to me I was very much aware of their increasing dread of the inevitability of my 'call up' papers.

It was a difficult time for my parents in many ways. In June the Corporation bought Nos. 7 and 8, Duke Street, and Father was notified that they planned to demolish Nos. 9 and 10 so that the view of the newly appointed Cathedral could be opened up. This meant that, although he would receive compensation, he would have to relinquish not only his business premises but also his home. The project was to cause him a great deal of worry over the next ten years although, in the end, everything turned out well.

I do not know whether he had ever thought that this might happen or whether it came as a complete surprise to him. It seems that the idea was not a new one as only recently I read a small booklet published in 1909 and entitled *Chelmsford With Its Surroundings - A Handbook for Residents and Visitors*. I was extremely interested to read H G Daniel's opinion of the view, or lack thereof, of St Mary's Church (as it then was) from the Duke Street.

"Several narrow passages connect Duke Street with the churchyard. It is an open question whether the church would gain or lose if it were less enclosed by the houses which surround it. We certainly cannot at present get a good view of the proportions of the building from any point. But the effect of grandeur that might be obtained if the houses were removed would, unfortunately, involve the

B H H in army uniform, 1918

loss of one of the churchyard's principal charms - its solitude. On a busy day, one may leave the crowded streets, turn into the shadows of the houses surrounding the church and find a haven of peacefulness, with only the sound of one's own footsteps on the flagged walks to break the stillness."

I watched the post anxiously and it was almost with a sense of relief that I was summoned to the Drill Hall for a medical examination on 26th July, just three days after my eighteenth birthday. After a brief look at me the Medical Officer pronounced me A1 and fit for active service. I was 'in'!

I was ordered to report to the Army tent in Westfields, Broomfield Road, on Wednesday, 7th August. How strange, I thought, that I should once again walk up Duke Street and along Broomfield Road with my mouth dry and my stomach turning over. It was almost ten years since my first day at the Grammar School when I had experienced just the same sinking feeling of apprehension and dread of what might lie ahead of me. I had thought I was grown up now - did adults really feel like this too?

Having reported at the stated time, there seemed nothing to do at Westfields but await further orders. It was getting quite late in the afternoon when about sixteen raw conscripts 'marched' down Broomfield Road to the railway station. We travelled by train to Brentwood and I shall never forget that short journey. I soon realised that most of the other lads were feeling every bit as nervous as I and that, for a couple from outlying rural areas, even the trauma of being in Chelmsford had been frightening. In fact one boy, already nick-named 'Sausage', was very uneasy about the traffic as we marched to the station. This was nothing compared to his misery on the train. He was literally terrified of the noise and speed of the train and alarmed the rest of us by howling in a bleating fashion all the way to Brentwood. Whenever another train passed us he would leap from his seat and bellow with anguish.

From Brentwood Station we had to march to Warley Barracks where we were to spend the night. That day I considered myself to be in a sort of limbo but I knew with certainty that this was my final day of being 'myself'. The next day would bring army clothes and kit, a rank and number, and almost certainly my departure from Essex for an unknown period of time. As I lay that night on a hard camp bed in a vast building like a warehouse, I knew that this was the end of an era for me. My childhood, my family, my schooldays, my home in Duke Street and all that was so familiar and dear to me flashed before my eyes with the utmost clarity. Would I ever return home to Chelmsford? I prayed that I would, and I fell asleep.

1896

Present Premises built 1929 (*Photographed 1946 still in war garb*)

1946

From the shop's Golden Jubilee material, showing 10 Duke Street